MISSOURI GENERAL CO.
CERTIFICATION EXAM PREP

By

Eric Davison, PhD

Copyright © 2024/2025

All Rights Reserved. This publication is protected by copyright. No part of this document may be reproduced, distributed, or transmitted in any form or by any means without prior written permission from the author.

This publication is for informational use only.

This publication is not intended to give legal advice. For legal advice, consult a legal professional.

This publication is not intended to diagnose, treat, or be construed as medical advice in any way.

Application of any information remains the professional responsibility of the practitioner.

The author does not assume and hereby disclaims any liability to any party for any loss, damage, and/or failure resulting from an error or omission, regardless of cause.

A PLUS EXAM REVIEW

Table of Contents
SECTION I: QUESTIONS

PART-ONE 5

Introduction to General Contractors Question 5

PART-TWO 11

Qualifications and Skills Question 11

PART-THREE 17

Types of Construction Projects Question 17

PART-FOUR 24

Responsibilities of General Contractors Question 24

PART-FIVE 30

Project Phases and General Contractor Involvement Question 30

PART-SIX 36

Building Codes and Regulations Question 36

PART-SEVEN 42

Contracting and Subcontracting Question 42

PART-EIGHT 48

Risk Management and Insurance Question 48

PART-NINE 54

Technology in Construction Question 54

PART-TEN 60

Emerging Trends and Innovations Question 60

PART-ELEVEN 67

Common Challenges Faced by General Contractors Question 67

PART-TWELVE 73

Case Studies Question 73

PART-FOURTEEN 77

Future Outlook of the Construction Industry Question 77

PART-FIFTEEN 84

General contractor Mathematics Calculations Question 84

SECTION II: ANSWERS

PART-ONE	96
Introduction to General Contractors Answer	96
PART-TWO	100
Qualifications and Skills Answer	100
PART-THREE	104
Types of Construction Projects Answer	104
PART-FOUR	108
Responsibilities of General Contractors Answer	108
PART-FIVE	112
Project Phases and General Contractor Involvement Answer	112
PART-SIX	116
Building Codes and Regulations Answer	116
PART-SEVEN	120
Contracting and Subcontracting Answer	120
PART-EIGHT	124
Risk Management and Insurance Answer	124
PART-NINE	128
Technology in Construction Answer	128
PART-TEN	132
Emerging Trends and Innovations Answer	132
PART-ELEVEN	136
Common Challenges Faced by General Contractors Answer	136
PART-TWELEVE	140
Case Studies Answer	140
PART-FOURTEEN	142
Future Outlook of the Construction Industry Answer	142
PART-FIFTEEN	146
General contractor Mathematics Calculations Answer	146

PART-ONE

Introduction to General Contractors Question

1. What is the minimum age requirement for obtaining a general contractor's license in Missouri?

    a. 18 years

    b. 21 years

    c. 25 years

    d. 30 years

2. Which department is responsible for licensing general contractors in Missouri?

    a. Missouri Department of Commerce and Insurance

    b. Missouri Department of Transportation

    c. Missouri Department of Labor

    d. Missouri Department of Revenue

3. How often must general contractors renew their licenses in Missouri?

    a. Every year

    b. Every two years

    c. Every three years

    d. Every five years

4. What type of insurance is typically required for licensed general contractors in Missouri?

    a. Health insurance

    b. Liability insurance

    c. Auto insurance

    d. Home insurance

5. Which of the following is a requirement for obtaining a general contractor's license in Missouri?

    a. High school diploma

    b. Bachelor's degree in construction management

    c. Completion of a qualifying examination

    d. Five years of experience in any field

6. In Missouri, what is the penalty for contracting without a license?

    a. Verbal warning

    b. Fine

    c. Community service

    d. Imprisonment

7. What is the primary purpose of the Missouri Contractor's License Board?

    a. To provide training for contractors

    b. To issue building permits

    c. To regulate and license contractors

    d. To conduct safety inspections

8. Which document outlines the terms and conditions of a construction project and is often required for obtaining a building permit?

    a. Project proposal

    b. Construction contract

    c. Bid bond

    d. Safety plan

9. What is the purpose of a bid bond in the construction industry?

    a. To ensure the contractor's safety practices

    b. To guarantee the contractor's performance

    c. To provide funds for the project

    d. To secure payment for subcontractors

10. In Missouri, which agency oversees workplace safety regulations for construction projects?

    a. Occupational Safety and Health Administration (OSHA)

    b. Missouri Department of Health and Senior Services

    c. Missouri Department of Labor

    d. Environmental Protection Agency (EPA)

11. What is a common requirement for subcontractors working on public projects in Missouri?

    a. Business license

    b. Specialized training

    c. Certification in first aid

    d. Performance bond

12. What type of projects typically require a general contractor's license in Missouri?

    a. Residential projects only

    b. Commercial projects only

    c. Both residential and commercial projects

    d. Public infrastructure projects

13. How can a general contractor in Missouri demonstrate financial responsibility?

    a. Submitting a personal bank statement

    b. Providing a credit report

    c. Obtaining a surety bond

    d. Offering collateral

14. What is the purpose of the Missouri Mechanic's Lien Law?

    a. To regulate contractors' fees

    b. To protect subcontractors' rights to payment

    c. To enforce safety regulations

    d. To establish building codes

15. What is the purpose of the pre-qualification process for contractors in Missouri?

    a. To determine eligibility for government contracts

    b. To assess environmental impact

    c. To establish safety guidelines

    d. To verify educational qualifications

16. Which entity issues building permits for construction projects in Missouri?

    a. Local municipalities

    b. Missouri Department of Transportation

    c. Missouri Contractor's License Board

    d. Federal Emergency Management Agency (FEMA)

17. What is the purpose of the Missouri Construction Lien Law?

    a. To regulate construction materials

    b. To establish safety standards

    c. To provide recourse for unpaid contractors and suppliers

    d. To determine property boundaries

18. Which of the following is a common requirement for obtaining a general contractor's license in Missouri?

    a. Completion of an apprenticeship program

    b. Submission of a business plan

    c. Passage of a criminal background check

    d. Ownership of a construction-related business for at least 10 years

19. What is the purpose of the Missouri Minimum Wage Law for public works projects?

    a. To establish a maximum wage for construction workers

    b. To ensure fair wages for workers on public construction projects

    c. To regulate overtime pay for contractors

    d. To set a minimum bid amount for contractors

20. What organization provides resources and support for continuing education for contractors in Missouri?

    a. Missouri Chamber of Commerce and Industry

    b. Missouri Department of Conservation

    c. Associated General Contractors (AGC) of Missouri

    d. Missouri State Board of Education

21. What is a common requirement for subcontractors working on state-funded projects in Missouri?

    a. Completion of a specialized training program

    b. Participation in a mentorship program

    c. Payment of a performance bond

    d. Certification as a Minority Business Enterprise (MBE)

22. Which of the following is a potential consequence of violating building codes in Missouri?

    a. Verbal warning

    b. Fine

    c. Community service

    d. Award of additional projects

23. In Missouri, what is the purpose of the Prevailing Wage Law?

    a. To establish a minimum wage for all construction workers

    b. To regulate working hours for contractors

    c. To ensure fair wages for workers on public construction projects

    d. To set maximum bid amounts for contractors

24. What is the purpose of the Missouri Division of Professional Registration in relation to contractors?

    a. To issue building permits

    b. To regulate construction materials

    c. To provide licensing for contractors

    d. To enforce environmental regulations

25. Which of the following is an essential step in the construction bidding process in Missouri?

    a. Providing inaccurate project estimates

    b. Submitting bids after the deadline

    c. Obtaining bid security

    d. Skipping the pre-bid meeting

PART-TWO

Qualifications and Skills Question

1. What is the minimum experience requirement for obtaining a general contractor's license in Missouri?

    a. 1 year

    b. 3 years

    c. 5 years

    d. 7 years

2. Which of the following degrees is often considered beneficial for a general contractor in Missouri?

    a. Engineering

    b. Business Administration

    c. Law

    d. Computer Science

3. What type of certification may enhance a general contractor's qualifications in Missouri?

    a. CPR Certification

    b. Project Management Professional (PMP)

    c. Microsoft Office Certification

    d. Food Handler Certification

4. In Missouri, what is the significance of being a licensed master electrician for a general contractor?

    a. It exempts them from electrical permits

    b. It allows them to perform electrical work

    c. It is a requirement for a general contractor license

    d. It provides tax benefits

5. What is a common skill required for effective project management by a general contractor in Missouri?

    a. Graphic design

    b. Programming

    c. Conflict resolution

    d. Musical composition

6. Which organization in Missouri provides professional development resources for general contractors?

    a. Missouri Department of Commerce and Insurance

    b. Associated General Contractors (AGC) of Missouri

    c. Missouri State Board of Education

    d. Missouri Department of Transportation

7. What is the purpose of obtaining a Lead-Based Paint Renovation License in Missouri?

    a. To perform plumbing work

    b. To work on projects involving lead-based paint

    c. To operate heavy machinery

    d. To conduct soil testing

8. Which of the following is a crucial aspect of effective communication for general contractors in Missouri?

    a. Speaking only in technical terms

    b. Providing vague instructions

    c. Clear and concise communication

    d. Ignoring stakeholder feedback

9. What role does a Safety Coordinator play in a general contractor's team in Missouri?

    a. Managing project finances

    b. Overseeing employee benefits

    c. Ensuring compliance with safety regulations

    d. Handling legal matters

10. What is the significance of a general contractor having strong negotiation skills in Missouri?

    a. It helps secure favorable insurance rates

    b. It aids in obtaining project financing

    c. It facilitates effective subcontractor agreements

    d. It reduces bonding requirements

11. In Missouri, what does it mean for a general contractor to be "bonded"?

    a. Having a secure financial investment

    b. Holding a surety bond

    c. Being insured against property damage

    d. Owning a construction license

12. What is the primary purpose of a general contractor's portfolio in Missouri?

    a. Showcasing personal achievements

    b. Demonstrating compliance with licensing requirements

    c. Highlighting completed projects and capabilities

    d. Providing a list of references

13. What is the primary role of a General Superintendent on a construction project in Missouri?

    a. Managing project finances

    b. Overseeing day-to-day operations

    c. Handling legal matters

    d. Ensuring compliance with zoning laws

14. Which of the following is a benefit of a general contractor having knowledge of sustainable construction practices in Missouri?

    a. Reduced project timelines

    b. Increased energy efficiency

    c. Higher bonding limits

    d. Exemption from licensing fees

15. What role does a Quality Control Manager play in the construction process in Missouri?

    a. Managing project finances

    b. Ensuring compliance with safety regulations

    c. Overseeing the quality of work

    d. Handling legal matters

16. How can a general contractor in Missouri stay updated on changes in building codes and regulations?

    a. Attend professional development workshops

    b. Ignore code updates

    c. Rely on subcontractors for information

    d. Update codes only when prompted by clients

17. What is a common skill required for successful budget management by a general contractor in Missouri?

    a. Impulse buying

    b. Micromanaging

    c. Cost estimation

    d. Ignoring financial reports

18. Why is it important for a general contractor in Missouri to have knowledge of construction contracts?

    a. To avoid legal liabilities

    b. To increase bonding limits

    c. To bypass building permits

    d. To eliminate the need for insurance

19. What role does a Safety Manual serve for a general contractor in Missouri?

    a. Documenting project milestones

    b. Providing guidelines for employee safety

    c. Listing financial transactions

    d. Describing architectural design details

20. In Missouri, what is the purpose of having a comprehensive Subcontractor Qualification Process?

    a. Avoiding any collaboration with subcontractors

    b. Streamlining the bidding process

    c. Increasing project delays

    d. Reducing risks associated with subcontractor performance

21. How can a general contractor in Missouri demonstrate a commitment to diversity and inclusion in their projects?

    a. Hiring only local subcontractors

    b. Utilizing environmentally friendly materials

    c. Participating in community outreach programs

    d. Ignoring equal opportunity employment practices

22. What is the purpose of obtaining a Commercial Driver's License (CDL) for a general contractor in Missouri?

    a. Operating heavy machinery

    b. Driving construction vehicles on public roads

    c. Navigating construction sites

    d. Transporting construction materials

23. How can a general contractor in Missouri enhance their leadership skills?

    a. Avoiding teamwork

    b. Ignoring feedback

    c. Participating in leadership training programs

    d. Discouraging employee growth

24. What is the purpose of a general contractor having knowledge of the Americans with Disabilities Act (ADA) in Missouri?

    a. Expediting permit approvals

    b. Bypassing safety regulations

    c. Ensuring accessibility in construction projects

    d. Eliminating the need for insurance

25. How can a general contractor in Missouri stay informed about emerging construction technologies?

    a. Avoiding technology adoption

    b. Relying solely on subcontractors for information

    c. Attending industry conferences and seminars

    d. Ignoring advancements in construction methods

PART-THREE

Types of Construction Projects Question

1. What type of construction project involves the building of residential homes, apartments, or condominiums?

    a. Commercial construction

    b. Industrial construction

    c. Residential construction

    d. Civil construction

2. Which construction project type focuses on the development of infrastructure such as roads, bridges, and utilities?

    a. Residential construction

    b. Civil construction

    c. Commercial construction

    d. Institutional construction

3. What type of construction project involves the construction of facilities for healthcare, education, or government purposes?

    a. Institutional construction

    b. Commercial construction

    c. Industrial construction

    d. Residential construction

4. Which construction project type is associated with manufacturing facilities, warehouses, and distribution centers?

    a. Industrial construction

    b. Civil construction

    c. Residential construction

    d. Commercial construction

5. What type of construction project involves the construction of retail spaces, office buildings, and shopping centers?

    a. Residential construction

    b. Institutional construction

    c. Commercial construction

    d. Civil construction

6. In Missouri, which type of construction project might involve the renovation or expansion of existing structures?

    a. New construction

    b. Greenfield construction

    c. Brownfield construction

    d. Retrofit construction

7. What type of construction project involves the use of environmentally friendly materials and practices to reduce the project's impact on the environment?

    a. Sustainable construction

    b. High-rise construction

    c. Mass timber construction

    d. Prefabricated construction

8. Which type of construction project involves the use of off-site manufacturing and assembly of building components before being transported to the construction site?

    a. Modular construction

    b. Traditional construction

    c. Design-Build construction

    d. Fast-track construction

9. What type of construction project involves the simultaneous design and construction phases, allowing for a faster project delivery?

    a. Design-Build construction

    b. Fast-track construction

    c. Traditional construction

    d. Construction management

10. In Missouri, which type of construction project might involve the redevelopment of previously used industrial or commercial sites?

    a. Greenfield construction

    b. Brownfield construction

    c. Sustainable construction

    d. Retrofit construction

11. Which construction project type involves the construction of high-rise buildings such as skyscrapers?

    a. Low-rise construction

    b. Mid-rise construction

    c. High-rise construction

    d. Subterranean construction

12. What type of construction project involves the use of large, solid wood panels for building construction?

    a. Mass timber construction

    b. Steel frame construction

    c. Concrete construction

    d. Timber frame construction

13. In Missouri, which construction project type might involve the construction of highways, bridges, and tunnels?

    a. Commercial construction

    b. Industrial construction

    c. Civil construction

    d. Institutional construction

14. What type of construction project involves the construction of facilities for entertainment, such as theaters, stadiums, and amusement parks?

    a. Entertainment construction

    b. Cultural construction

    c. Recreational construction

    d. Institutional construction

15. Which construction project type involves the construction of structures below the ground surface, such as basements and subway stations?

    a. Above-ground construction

    b. Subterranean construction

    c. Elevated construction

    d. Ground-level construction

16. What type of construction project involves the construction of structures for religious purposes, such as churches, mosques, and temples?

    a. Religious construction

    b. Sacred construction

    c. Spiritual construction

    d. Institutional construction

17. In Missouri, which type of construction project might involve the restoration of historic buildings or landmarks?

    a. Adaptive reuse construction

    b. Preservation construction

    c. Historical construction

    d. Heritage construction

18. What type of construction project involves the construction of facilities for research, development, and scientific purposes?

    a. Laboratory construction

    b. Scientific construction

    c. Research construction

    d. Institutional construction

19. Which construction project type involves the construction of structures for the storage of goods, such as warehouses and distribution centers?

    a. Storage construction

    b. Logistics construction

    c. Warehousing construction

    d. Distribution construction

20. What type of construction project involves the creation of specialized spaces for the production of goods or manufacturing processes?

    a. Production construction

    b. Manufacturing construction

    c. Industrial construction

    d. Assembly construction

21. In Missouri, which type of construction project might involve the construction of public parks, sports fields, or playgrounds?

    a. Green construction

    b. Park construction

    c. Recreation construction

    d. Landscape construction

22. What type of construction project involves the construction of facilities for the arts, such as museums, galleries, and theaters?

    a. Cultural construction

    b. Arts construction

    c. Fine arts construction

    d. Entertainment construction

23. Which construction project type involves the construction of structures for educational purposes, such as schools and universities?

    a. Educational construction

    b. Learning construction

    c. Academic construction

    d. Institutional construction

24. What type of construction project involves the construction of structures for the storage and treatment of water and wastewater?

    a. Water construction

    b. Environmental construction

    c. Infrastructure construction

    d. Water and wastewater construction

25. In Missouri, which type of construction project might involve the construction of facilities for the hospitality industry, such as hotels and resorts?

    a. Hospitality construction

    b. Hotel construction

    c. Resort construction

    d. Lodging construction

PART-FOUR

Responsibilities of General Contractors Question

1. What is the primary responsibility of a general contractor in Missouri?

    a. Designing structures

    b. Managing construction projects

    c. Inspecting electrical systems

    d. Handling legal documentation

2. In Missouri, which entity typically issues licenses to general contractors?

    a. Department of Transportation

    b. Department of Agriculture

    c. Missouri Division of Professional Registration

    d. Environmental Protection Agency

3. What is a common requirement for obtaining a general contractor's license in Missouri?

    a. Passing a written exam

    b. Owning a construction company for 10 years

    c. Having a degree in architecture

    d. Volunteering in community projects

4. Which of the following is NOT typically a responsibility of a general contractor in Missouri?

    a. Hiring subcontractors

    b. Ensuring compliance with building codes

    c. Marketing construction services

    d. Providing medical services to workers

5. In Missouri, what document outlines the terms and conditions of a construction project and is signed by both parties involved?

    a. Construction manual

    b. Building code

    c. Construction contract

    d. Blueprint

6. What is the purpose of a performance bond for a general contractor in Missouri?

    a. Ensuring compliance with building codes

    b. Providing insurance for workers

    c. Guaranteeing completion of the project

    d. Financing construction materials

7. Which agency in Missouri is responsible for enforcing building codes?

    a. Department of Natural Resources

    b. Department of Conservation

    c. Department of Labor and Industrial Relations

    d. Department of Economic Development

8. What is the role of a general contractor in ensuring workplace safety on a construction site in Missouri?

    a. Conducting medical examinations

    b. Providing personal protective equipment (PPE)

    c. Handling worker compensation claims

    d. Marketing safety seminars

9. What type of insurance coverage is commonly required for general contractors in Missouri?

    a. Life insurance

    b. Auto insurance

    c. Builder's risk insurance

    d. Travel insurance

10. What does the "Missouri Prompt Pay Act" address in relation to general contractors?

    a. Minimum wage for construction workers

    b. Timely payment to subcontractors

    c. Environmental regulations

    d. Licensing requirements

11. What is the significance of a lien waiver in the construction industry in Missouri?

    a. Grants permission to use specific materials

    b. Releases the right to file a mechanics lien

    c. Allows unlimited changes to the project scope

    d. Authorizes demolition of existing structures

12. What agency oversees apprenticeship programs for the construction industry in Missouri?

    a. Missouri Department of Higher Education

    b. Missouri Department of Elementary and Secondary Education

    c. Missouri Division of Workforce Development

    d. Missouri Department of Revenue

13. How often are general contractors in Missouri required to renew their licenses?

    a. Every 2 years

    b. Every 5 years

    c. Every 10 years

    d. No renewal required

14. In Missouri, what is the purpose of the "Prevailing Wage" law?

    a. Establishing minimum wages for construction workers

    b. Regulating working hours for contractors

    c. Mandating specific construction techniques

    d. Setting prices for construction materials

15. What role does a general contractor play in obtaining necessary permits for a construction project in Missouri?

    a. Drafting architectural plans

    b. Communicating with local authorities

    c. Conducting soil tests

    d. Supervising building inspections

16. How does the "Right to Repair Act" impact general contractors in Missouri?

    a. It requires contractors to provide free repairs

    b. It limits the time frame for filing construction defect claims

    c. It mandates specific repair methods

    d. It bans certain construction materials

17. What is the purpose of a certificate of insurance for a general contractor in Missouri?

    a. Authorizing construction materials purchase

    b. Certifying completion of the project

    c. Confirming insurance coverage

    d. Approving architectural designs

18. Which of the following is NOT a typical document in the bidding process for a construction project in Missouri?

    a. Bid bond

    b. Surety bond

    c. Bid proposal

    d. Environmental impact statement

19. What does the "Missouri Contractors' Preference Law" aim to achieve?

    a. Prioritizing out-of-state contractors

    b. Giving preference to local contractors

    c. Banning certain construction methods

    d. Limiting the use of subcontractors

20. In Missouri, what agency is responsible for handling workers' compensation claims in the construction industry?

    a. Department of Insurance, Financial Institutions & Professional Registration

    b. Department of Economic Development

    c. Department of Labor and Industrial Relations

    d. Department of Health and Senior Services

21. What is a "Substantial Completion" certificate in the context of construction projects in Missouri?

    a. An invoice for completed work

    b. A certificate of occupancy

    c. A notice to proceed

    d. A declaration of project abandonment

22. How does the "Missouri Sunshine Law" impact general contractors?

    a. It mandates the use of solar energy in construction projects

    b. It requires contractors to disclose project budgets

    c. It ensures transparency in government-related activities

    d. It limits working hours on construction sites

23. What is the purpose of a change order in a construction project in Missouri?

    a. Altering the project's fundamental design

    b. Modifying the construction contract terms

    c. Changing the project's location

    d. Switching subcontractors

24. What role does a general contractor play in dispute resolution on a construction project in Missouri?

    a. Arbitrating conflicts between subcontractors

    b. Ignoring disputes to avoid liability

    c. Filing lawsuits against clients

    d. Escalating conflicts without intervention

25. How can a general contractor in Missouri protect themselves from potential legal disputes?

    a. Ignoring legal contracts

    b. Avoiding insurance coverage

    c. Communicating clearly with all parties

    d. Refusing to obtain necessary permits

PART-FIVE

Project Phases and General Contractor Involvement Question

1. During which project phase does the general contractor typically become involved in Missouri?

    a. Conceptual Phase

    b. Design Phase

    c. Construction Phase

    d. Closeout Phase

2. What is the primary goal of the Pre-Construction Phase in Missouri projects?

    a. Finalizing construction plans

    b. Awarding contracts to subcontractors

    c. Establishing project objectives and parameters

    d. Completing construction activities

3. What document outlines the project scope, schedule, and budget during the Pre-Construction Phase in Missouri?

    a. Bid proposal

    b. Construction contract

    c. Project management plan

    d. Surety bond

4. What role does the general contractor play during the Design Phase in Missouri projects?

    a. Finalizing architectural designs

    b. Providing input on constructability and costs

    c. Obtaining necessary permits

    d. Conducting safety inspections

5. In Missouri, what is the purpose of the "Request for Proposal (RFP)" document during the Bid Phase?

    a. Inviting contractors to submit bids

    b. Describing project objectives

    c. Finalizing construction plans

    d. Obtaining project financing

6. Which phase involves the actual physical construction of the project in Missouri?

    a. Design Phase

    b. Bid Phase

    c. Pre-Construction Phase

    d. Construction Phase

7. What is the purpose of a "Notice to Proceed" during the Construction Phase in Missouri?

    a. Authorizing construction to begin

    b. Notifying about design changes

    c. Issuing a stop-work order

    d. Announcing project completion

8. What is the primary responsibility of the general contractor during the Construction Phase in Missouri?

    a. Creating architectural designs

    b. Managing the construction process

    c. Obtaining project financing

    d. Drafting legal contracts

9. What document outlines the terms, conditions, and responsibilities of the parties involved in the construction project in Missouri?

    a. Project schedule

    b. Construction contract

    c. Bid proposal

    d. Architectural drawings

10. During the Construction Phase in Missouri, what is the purpose of a "Change Order"?

    a. Altering the project's fundamental design

    b. Modifying the construction contract terms

    c. Changing the project's location

    d. Switching subcontractors

11. What is the primary focus of the Post-Construction Phase in Missouri projects?

    a. Finalizing construction plans

    b. Conducting safety inspections

    c. Completing punch lists and inspections

    d. Awarding contracts to subcontractors

12. In Missouri, what document signifies the completion of the construction project and the owner's acceptance of the work?

    a. Notice to Proceed

    b. Certificate of Substantial Completion

    c. Change Order

    d. Request for Proposal (RFP)

13. What is the purpose of the "Final Completion Certificate" in Missouri projects?

    a. Authorizing additional construction work

    b. Confirming the completion of all project work

    c. Issuing a stop-work order

    d. Providing approval for design changes

14. What role does the general contractor play during the Warranty Phase in Missouri?

    a. Conducting safety inspections

    b. Extending project warranties

    c. Finalizing construction plans

    d. Marketing construction services

15. How does the "Retention" process impact payments to subcontractors in Missouri projects?

    a. It accelerates payment schedules

    b. It withholds a portion of payments until project completion

    c. It eliminates the need for payment bonds

    d. It guarantees early project completion

16. What is the purpose of the "Punch List" in Missouri construction projects?

    a. A list of construction materials needed

    b. A list of final project inspections

    c. A list of incomplete or deficient work

    d. A list of approved subcontractors

17. What is the significance of the "Certificate of Occupancy" in Missouri construction projects?

    a. Authorizing construction materials purchase

    b. Certifying completion of the project

    c. Confirming insurance coverage

    d. Approving architectural designs

18. How does the "Closeout Phase" contribute to project completion in Missouri?

    a. Initiating construction activities

    b. Completing punch lists and inspections

    c. Authorizing additional construction work

    d. Finalizing architectural designs

19. What is the purpose of the "As-Built Drawings" in Missouri construction projects?

    a. Illustrating the project's initial design

    b. Documenting changes made during construction

    c. Identifying potential safety hazards

    d. Creating a marketing brochure

20. What is the primary goal of the "Project Closeout" process in Missouri?

    a. Initiating construction activities

    b. Documenting project changes

    c. Finalizing contractual obligations

    d. Obtaining project financing

21. How does the "Retention" process impact general contractors in Missouri?

    a. It accelerates payment schedules

    b. It withholds a portion of payments until project completion

    c. It eliminates the need for payment bonds

    d. It guarantees early project completion

22. What is the purpose of a "Project Kickoff Meeting" in Missouri construction projects?

    a. Finalizing construction plans

    b. Awarding contracts to subcontractors

    c. Discussing project objectives and expectations

    d. Issuing a stop-work order

23. How does the "Pay Application" process work in Missouri construction projects?

    a. It ensures timely payment to subcontractors

    b. It eliminates the need for project financing

    c. It accelerates the construction timeline

    d. It issues final project acceptance

24. What role does the general contractor play in obtaining necessary permits for a construction project in Missouri?

    a. Drafting architectural plans

    b. Communicating with local authorities

    c. Conducting soil tests

    d. Supervising building inspections

25. What is the primary objective of the "Commissioning" process in Missouri construction projects?

    a. Achieving LEED certification

    b. Testing and verifying systems for proper functionality

    c. Conducting safety inspections

    d. Finalizing architectural designs

PART-SIX

Building Codes and Regulations Question

1. Which agency in Missouri is responsible for adopting and enforcing building codes statewide?

    a. Missouri Department of Natural Resources

    b. Missouri Division of Professional Registration

    c. Missouri Department of Economic Development

    d. Local municipalities and counties

2. What is the purpose of building codes in Missouri?

    a. To limit construction materials

    b. To stifle architectural creativity

    c. To ensure public safety and welfare

    d. To increase construction costs

3. In Missouri, which document contains the specific requirements for construction and design of buildings?

    a. Construction contracts

    b. Bid proposals

    c. Building codes

    d. Architectural drawings

4. How often are building codes typically updated in Missouri?

    a. Every 2 years

    b. Every 5 years

    c. Every 10 years

    d. No regular update schedule

5. What is the purpose of a building permit in Missouri?

    a. To authorize demolition of existing structures

    b. To grant permission to use specific materials

    c. To approve architectural designs

    d. To ensure compliance with building codes

6. Which of the following construction projects in Missouri would likely require a building permit?

    a. Building a treehouse in a backyard

    b. Installing a new light fixture indoors

    c. Painting the exterior of a house

    d. Adding a room to an existing home

7. What is the consequence of proceeding with construction without obtaining the required building permits in Missouri?

    a. A discount on permit fees

    b. No impact on the project

    c. Fines and penalties

    d. Immediate project approval

8. In Missouri, what type of inspections are typically conducted during different phases of construction?

    a. Architectural inspections only

    b. Final inspections only

    c. Pre-construction inspections only

    d. Various inspections throughout the construction process

9. What is a variance in the context of building codes in Missouri?

    a. A penalty for code violations

    b. A waiver from specific code requirements

    c. A mandatory inspection

    d. A type of construction material

10. What agency in Missouri is responsible for granting variances from building code requirements?

    a. Missouri Department of Conservation

    b. Missouri Division of Professional Registration

    c. Local board of appeals or zoning board

    d. Missouri Department of Transportation

11. How does the Americans with Disabilities Act (ADA) impact building codes in Missouri?

    a. It increases construction costs

    b. It has no impact on building codes

    c. It mandates accessibility standards

    d. It limits architectural creativity

12. What role does a general contractor play in ensuring compliance with building codes in Missouri?

    a. Designing architectural plans

    b. Conducting environmental impact assessments

    c. Obtaining building permits

    d. Administering health and safety programs

13. What is the purpose of the "Certificate of Occupancy" in Missouri?

    a. Authorizing construction materials purchase

    b. Certifying completion of the project

    c. Confirming insurance coverage

    d. Approving architectural designs

14. In Missouri, what is the "International Building Code (IBC)" primarily concerned with?

    a. Plumbing and electrical systems

    b. Structural and fire safety

    c. Environmental sustainability

    d. Architectural aesthetics

15. What is the purpose of the "Energy Conservation Code" in Missouri?

    a. Mandating specific construction materials

    b. Regulating working hours for contractors

    c. Ensuring energy-efficient building practices

    d. Establishing minimum wages for construction workers

16. How does the "Missouri State Fire Code" impact construction projects in the state?

    a. It regulates plumbing and electrical systems

    b. It sets standards for environmental sustainability

    c. It addresses fire prevention and safety measures

    d. It establishes architectural design criteria

17. What is the purpose of the "Missouri Accessibility Code" in construction projects?

    a. Regulating working hours for contractors

    b. Ensuring compliance with environmental regulations

    c. Mandating accessibility standards

    d. Establishing minimum wages for construction workers

18. How does the "International Plumbing Code (IPC)" impact construction projects in Missouri?

    a. It regulates plumbing and electrical systems

    b. It sets standards for environmental sustainability

    c. It addresses fire prevention and safety measures

    d. It establishes criteria for plumbing installations

19. What is the purpose of the "Missouri Lead Abatement Code" in construction projects?

    a. Regulating working hours for contractors

    b. Ensuring compliance with environmental regulations

    c. Addressing lead-based paint hazards

    d. Establishing minimum wages for construction workers

20. How does the "International Mechanical Code (IMC)" impact construction projects in Missouri?

    a. It regulates plumbing and electrical systems

    b. It sets standards for environmental sustainability

    c. It addresses fire prevention and safety measures

    d. It establishes criteria for mechanical installations

21. What is the role of the general contractor in addressing building code violations on a construction site in Missouri?

    a. Ignoring violations to save costs

    b. Immediately correcting violations

    c. Blaming subcontractors for violations

    d. Reporting violations to the client

22. How does the "Missouri Structural Code" contribute to construction safety?

    a. It regulates plumbing and electrical systems

    b. It sets standards for environmental sustainability

    c. It addresses structural safety in buildings

    d. It establishes criteria for architectural designs

23. What is the purpose of the "International Fuel Gas Code (IFGC)" in construction projects in Missouri?

    a. Regulating plumbing and electrical systems

    b. Ensuring compliance with environmental regulations

    c. Addressing fire prevention and safety measures

    d. Establishing criteria for fuel gas installations

24. How can a general contractor stay informed about updates to building codes in Missouri?

    a. Ignoring code updates for cost savings

    b. Relying solely on subcontractors for information

    c. Attending code training sessions and seminars

    d. Waiting for local authorities to notify them

25. How does the "Uniform Plumbing Code (UPC)" impact construction projects in Missouri?

    a. It regulates plumbing and electrical systems

    b. It sets standards for environmental sustainability

    c. It addresses fire prevention and safety measures

    d. It establishes criteria for plumbing installations

PART-SEVEN

Contracting and Subcontracting Question

1. In Missouri, what is a common legal document that outlines the terms and conditions of a construction project and is signed by both the owner and the general contractor?

    a. Business license

    b. Construction contract

    c. Environmental impact statement

    d. Insurance policy

2. What is the purpose of a bid proposal in the context of construction contracting in Missouri?

    a. Authorizing construction to begin

    b. Certifying completion of the project

    c. Inviting contractors to submit bids

    d. Confirming insurance coverage

3. In Missouri, what type of contract compensates the general contractor based on a percentage of the total project cost?

    a. Lump sum contract

    b. Cost-plus contract

    c. Fixed-price contract

    d. Unit price contract

4. What is the primary advantage of a lump sum contract for a general contractor in Missouri?

    a. Guaranteed maximum price

    b. Flexibility in project changes

    c. Faster project completion

    d. Lower overall project cost

5. In Missouri, what is the purpose of a performance bond for a general contractor?

    a. Providing insurance for workers

    b. Guaranteeing completion of the project

    c. Financing construction materials

    d. Ensuring compliance with building codes

6. How does the "Missouri Prompt Pay Act" impact payment practices in construction contracts?

    a. Delays payment to subcontractors

    b. Requires prompt payment to subcontractors

    c. Sets a fixed payment schedule

    d. Eliminates payment for overtime work

7. In Missouri, what is the purpose of a lien waiver in the construction industry?

    a. Grants permission to use specific materials

    b. Releases the right to file a mechanics lien

    c. Approves changes to the project scope

    d. Authorizes demolition of existing structures

8. What is the significance of a retainage clause in a construction contract in Missouri?

    a. Authorizes additional construction work

    b. Specifies the project completion date

    c. Withholds a portion of payments until project completion

    d. Limits the scope of work

9. In Missouri, what type of contract compensates the general contractor based on the actual costs incurred, plus a fixed fee for profit and overhead?

    a. Lump sum contract

    b. Cost-plus contract

    c. Fixed-price contract

    d. Unit price contract

10. What is the primary purpose of the "Subcontractor Default Insurance (SDI)" in Missouri?

    a. Protecting subcontractors from default

    b. Protecting general contractors from defaulting subcontractors

    c. Eliminating the need for performance bonds

    d. Reducing project costs

11. How does the "Missouri Contractors' Preference Law" impact subcontracting practices?

    a. Prioritizes out-of-state subcontractors

    b. Gives preference to local subcontractors

    c. Bans certain subcontracting methods

    d. Limits the use of subcontractors

12. What role does a general contractor play in the subcontractor selection process in Missouri?

    a. Issuing building permits

    b. Approving architectural designs

    c. Hiring and coordinating subcontractors

    d. Conducting environmental impact assessments

13. In Missouri, what is a common requirement for subcontractors to participate in a public construction project?

    a. Ownership of a construction company for 20 years

    b. Completion of a medical examination

    c. Submission of a bid proposal

    d. Passing a pre-qualification process

14. What is the purpose of a bid bond in Missouri construction contracts?

    a. Guaranteeing performance of the project

    b. Providing insurance for workers

    c. Financing construction materials

    d. Certifying completion of the project

15. How does the "Missouri Sunshine Law" impact subcontracting in public construction projects?

    a. It mandates the use of solar energy

    b. It requires subcontractors to disclose project budgets

    c. It ensures transparency in government-related activities

    d. It limits working hours for subcontractors

16. What is the purpose of the "Bid Protest" process in Missouri construction contracts?

    a. Approving changes to the project scope

    b. Challenging the awarding of a contract

    c. Issuing stop-work orders

    d. Authorizing additional construction work

17. How does the "Missouri Minority Business Enterprises (MBE) Program" support subcontracting in construction projects?

    a. Excludes minority-owned businesses from subcontracting

    b. Provides financial incentives for minority-owned subcontractors

    c. Requires subcontractors to disclose project budgets

    d. Limits the use of minority-owned subcontractors

18. What is the purpose of the "Notice to Proceed" in subcontracting on a construction project in Missouri?

    a. Authorizing construction to begin

    b. Notifying about design changes

    c. Issuing a stop-work order

    d. Announcing project completion

19. What is the primary responsibility of a subcontractor in Missouri regarding safety on the construction site?

    a. Ignoring safety regulations to save time

    b. Leaving safety measures to the general contractor

    c. Complying with safety regulations and guidelines

    d. Filing lawsuits against the owner

20. How does the "Retention" process impact payments to subcontractors in Missouri construction projects?

    a. Accelerates payment schedules

    b. Withholds a portion of payments until project completion

    c. Eliminates the need for payment bonds

    d. Guarantees early project completion

21. What is the purpose of a "Subcontractor Agreement" in Missouri construction projects?

    a. Approving changes to the project scope

    b. Certifying completion of the project

    c. Establishing the terms between the general contractor and subcontractor

    d. Authorizing additional construction work

22. How can a subcontractor in Missouri protect themselves from non-payment issues?

    a. Ignoring lien rights

    b. Avoiding written contracts

    c. Filing lawsuits immediately

    d. Filing a mechanics lien

23. What is the purpose of the "Subcontractor Performance Bond" in Missouri?

    a. Certifying completion of the project

    b. Providing insurance for subcontractors

    c. Guaranteeing performance of subcontracted work

    d. Financing construction materials

24. How does the "Subcontractor Default Insurance (SDI)" benefit subcontractors in Missouri?

    a. Increases project costs for subcontractors

    b. Provides protection against default by subcontractors

    c. Eliminates the need for performance bonds

    d. Limits subcontractor liability

25. What role does a general contractor play in dispute resolution between subcontractors on a construction project in Missouri?

    a. Ignoring disputes to avoid liability

    b. Arbitrating conflicts between subcontractors

    c. Filing lawsuits against subcontractors

    d. Escalating conflicts without intervention

PART-EIGHT

Risk Management and Insurance Question

1. What is the purpose of liability insurance for a general contractor in Missouri?

    a. Protecting the construction materials

    b. Covering damage to completed projects

    c. Providing coverage for bodily injury or property damage claims

    d. Ensuring compliance with building codes

2. In Missouri, what type of insurance protects a general contractor against financial losses due to project delays or interruptions?

    a. Liability insurance

    b. Builder's risk insurance

    c. Workers' compensation insurance

    d. Professional liability insurance

3. How does workers' compensation insurance benefit a general contractor in Missouri?

    a. Protecting against project delays

    b. Providing coverage for bodily injury to employees

    c. Covering damage to completed projects

    d. Ensuring compliance with building codes

4. What is the purpose of professional liability insurance for a general contractor in Missouri?

    a. Covering damage to completed projects

    b. Protecting against project delays

    c. Providing coverage for design errors or negligence

    d. Ensuring compliance with building codes

5. In Missouri, how can a general contractor mitigate the risk of subcontractor default on a project?

    a. Ignoring the financial stability of subcontractors

    b. Relying solely on contracts without performance bonds

    c. Implementing a Subcontractor Default Insurance (SDI) program

    d. Avoiding written contracts with subcontractors

6. What is the purpose of a surety bond for a general contractor in Missouri?

    a. Providing coverage for bodily injury

    b. Certifying completion of the project

    c. Covering damage to completed projects

    d. Guaranteeing performance of contractual obligations

7. How does risk transfer through indemnification clauses in contracts benefit a general contractor in Missouri?

    a. Increases project costs

    b. Shifts liability to subcontractors

    c. Eliminates the need for insurance

    d. Limits the scope of work

8. What role does a Certificate of Insurance (COI) play in risk management for a general contractor in Missouri?

    a. Authorizing construction to begin

    b. Certifying completion of the project

    c. Providing proof of insurance coverage from subcontractors

    d. Ensuring compliance with building codes

9. How does a general contractor in Missouri benefit from having a comprehensive safety program in place?

    a. Delays project completion

    b. Reduces the risk of accidents and injuries

    c. Increases insurance premiums

    d. Shifts responsibility to subcontractors

10. What is the primary purpose of a hold harmless clause in a contract for a general contractor in Missouri?

    a. Certifying completion of the project

    b. Eliminating all risk and liability

    c. Ensuring compliance with building codes

    d. Allocating certain risks to another party

11. How does subcontractor prequalification contribute to risk management for a general contractor in Missouri?

    a. Increases the likelihood of subcontractor default

    b. Accelerates project completion

    c. Shifts all risks to subcontractors

    d. Assesses the financial stability and capability of subcontractors

12. In Missouri, how does the "Safety and Health Achievement Recognition Program (SHARP)" impact risk management for a general contractor?

    a. Increases the risk of accidents

    b. Provides discounts on insurance premiums

    c. Eliminates the need for insurance

    d. Shifts responsibility to subcontractors

13. What is the purpose of an insurance policy deductible for a general contractor in Missouri?

    a. Increasing insurance premiums

    b. Eliminating the need for insurance

    c. Shifting all risks to subcontractors

    d. Sharing the financial responsibility with the insurance company

14. How does the use of subcontractor default insurance (SDI) impact risk management for a general contractor in Missouri?

    a. Increases the risk of subcontractor default

    b. Shifts financial responsibility to the general contractor

    c. Provides protection against financial losses from subcontractor default

    d. Eliminates the need for insurance

15. What role does contractual indemnity play in risk management for a general contractor in Missouri?

    a. Increases project costs

    b. Eliminates all risk and liability

    c. Transfers liability to the project owner

    d. Allocates certain risks to another party

16. How does the use of risk assessment tools benefit a general contractor in Missouri?

    a. Increases project costs

    b. Eliminates all project risks

    c. Identifies and evaluates potential risks

    d. Shifts responsibility to subcontractors

17. What is the purpose of a waiver of subrogation in an insurance policy for a general contractor in Missouri?

    a. Increases project costs

    b. Eliminates all risk and liability

    c. Allows the insurance company to pursue legal action against subcontractors

    d. Prevents the insurance company from suing subcontractors

18. How does a general contractor in Missouri benefit from having a crisis management plan in place?

    a. Increases the risk of accidents

    b. Accelerates project completion

    c. Reduces the impact of unforeseen events

    d. Shifts responsibility to subcontractors

19. How does a project owner transferring risk through insurance requirements impact a general contractor in Missouri?

    a. Increases insurance premiums

    b. Shifts responsibility to subcontractors

    c. Reduces the need for insurance

    d. Requires the general contractor to comply with specified insurance requirements

20. What is the primary purpose of the "Missouri Builders' Risk Insurance Act"?

    a. Regulating workers' compensation insurance

    b. Setting standards for professional liability insurance

    c. Defining requirements for builder's risk insurance

    d. Eliminating the need for insurance

21. How does the use of a risk register benefit a general contractor in Missouri?

    a. Increases project costs

    b. Eliminates all project risks

    c. Provides a systematic approach to identify, assess, and manage risks

    d. Shifts responsibility to subcontractors

22. How does the "Economic Loss Doctrine" impact risk management for a general contractor in Missouri?

    a. Eliminates the need for insurance

    b. Prevents recovery of economic losses through tort claims

    c. Shifts all risks to subcontractors

    d. Increases project costs

23. What is the purpose of a risk management plan for a general contractor in Missouri?

    a. Increases project costs

    b. Eliminates all project risks

    c. Provides a structured approach to identify, assess, and respond to risks

    d. Shifts responsibility to subcontractors

24. How does the use of performance bonds benefit a general contractor in Missouri?

    a. Increases project costs

    b. Certifies completion of the project

    c. Eliminates the need for insurance

    d. Shifts all risks to subcontractors

25. What role does insurance coverage play in the risk management of a general contractor in Missouri?

    a. Shifts all risks to subcontractors

    b. Eliminates the need for a risk management plan

    c. Provides financial protection against unforeseen events

    d. Increases project costs

PART-NINE

Technology in Construction Question

1. How can Building Information Modeling (BIM) benefit a general contractor in Missouri?

    a. Increases project costs

    b. Provides a 3D representation of the construction project

    c. Eliminates the need for project scheduling

    d. Shifts responsibility to subcontractors

2. In Missouri, what role does drones or Unmanned Aerial Vehicles (UAVs) play in construction projects?

    a. Facilitating communication among workers

    b. Aiding in site surveys, inspections, and monitoring

    c. Replacing traditional construction materials

    d. Reducing the need for project documentation

3. How does the use of construction management software benefit a general contractor in Missouri?

    a. Increases project costs

    b. Automates project management tasks

    c. Eliminates the need for communication

    d. Shifts responsibility to subcontractors

4. What is the purpose of Augmented Reality (AR) in construction in Missouri?

    a. Enhancing communication through virtual meetings

    b. Providing real-time project cost analysis

    c. Overlapping virtual information onto the physical construction site

    d. Replacing traditional safety measures

5. In Missouri, how can prefabrication and modular construction methods impact a construction project?
    a. Increases project costs
    b. Slows down construction timelines
    c. Accelerates project schedules and reduces on-site work
    d. Eliminates the need for project documentation

6. What role does 3D printing play in construction projects in Missouri?
    a. Enhancing project communication
    b. Creating physical objects layer by layer from digital models
    c. Replacing traditional construction tools
    d. Eliminating the need for project collaboration

7. How does the use of Virtual Reality (VR) benefit a general contractor in Missouri?
    a. Increases project costs
    b. Enhances collaboration among project stakeholders
    c. Eliminates the need for project scheduling
    d. Shifts responsibility to subcontractors

8. What is the significance of laser scanning technology in construction in Missouri?
    a. Enhancing communication through virtual meetings
    b. Aiding in accurate as-built documentation and site measurements
    c. Replacing traditional safety measures
    d. Reducing the need for project collaboration

9. How does the use of mobile construction apps benefit a general contractor in Missouri?
    a. Increases project costs
    b. Streamlines communication and access to project information
    c. Eliminates the need for project documentation
    d. Shifts responsibility to subcontractors

10. In Missouri, how can Geographic Information System (GIS) technology be utilized in construction projects?

    a. Enhancing project communication

    b. Aiding in site selection and analysis

    c. Replacing traditional construction materials

    d. Eliminating the need for project scheduling

11. What is the purpose of Real-time Project Collaboration Platforms in construction in Missouri?

    a. Increasing project costs

    b. Streamlining communication and collaboration among project team members

    c. Eliminating the need for project scheduling

    d. Shifting responsibility to subcontractors

12. How does the use of Construction Robotics impact construction projects in Missouri?

    a. Enhancing project communication

    b. Automating repetitive and labor-intensive tasks

    c. Replacing traditional construction tools

    d. Eliminating the need for project collaboration

13. What role does Internet of Things (IoT) technology play in construction projects in Missouri?

    a. Enhancing project communication

    b. Connecting and collecting data from construction equipment and devices

    c. Replacing traditional construction materials

    d. Eliminating the need for project scheduling

14. How does the use of Wearable Technology benefit construction workers in Missouri?

    a. Increases project costs

    b. Provides real-time health monitoring and safety alerts

    c. Eliminates the need for project documentation

    d. Shifts responsibility to subcontractors

15. What is the purpose of a Construction Project Management Information System (PMIS) in Missouri?

    a. Increasing project costs

    b. Streamlining project management tasks and processes

    c. Eliminating the need for project scheduling

    d. Shifting responsibility to subcontractors

16. How can Machine Learning and Artificial Intelligence (AI) be utilized in construction projects in Missouri?

    a. Enhancing project communication

    b. Analyzing data to predict project outcomes and optimize decision-making

    c. Replacing traditional construction tools

    d. Eliminating the need for project collaboration

17. In Missouri, how does the use of RFID technology benefit construction site management?

    a. Enhancing project communication

    b. Tracking and managing construction materials and equipment

    c. Replacing traditional safety measures

    d. Reducing the need for project collaboration

18. What is the significance of Cloud Computing in construction projects in Missouri?

    a. Enhancing project communication

    b. Providing a centralized platform for data storage and collaboration

    c. Replacing traditional construction materials

    d. Eliminating the need for project scheduling

19. How does the use of Advanced Surveying Technologies benefit construction projects in Missouri?

    a. Enhancing project communication

    b. Providing precise and detailed site measurements

    c. Replacing traditional safety measures

    d. Reducing the need for project collaboration

20. What role does Project Visualization Software play in construction projects in Missouri?

    a. Increasing project costs

    b. Enhancing visualization of project plans and designs

    c. Eliminating the need for project documentation

    d. Shifting responsibility to subcontractors

21. How can the use of Automated Equipment and Robotics benefit construction projects in Missouri?

    a. Enhancing project communication

    b. Increasing the speed and efficiency of construction tasks

    c. Replacing traditional construction tools

    d. Eliminating the need for project collaboration

22. What is the purpose of Environmental Monitoring Technology in construction projects in Missouri?

    a. Enhancing project communication

    b. Monitoring and managing environmental impacts

    c. Replacing traditional safety measures

    d. Reducing the need for project collaboration

23. In Missouri, how can Smart Construction Equipment improve project efficiency?

    a. Enhancing project communication

    b. Providing real-time data and diagnostics for construction equipment

    c. Replacing traditional construction materials

    d. Eliminating the need for project scheduling

24. How does the use of Collaborative Project Delivery Methods benefit construction projects in Missouri?

    a. Increases project costs

    b. Enhances collaboration among project stakeholders

    c. Eliminates the need for project documentation

    d. Shifts responsibility to subcontractors

25. What role does Augmented Reality (AR) play in training construction workers in Missouri?

    a. Enhancing project communication

    b. Providing immersive training experiences for construction tasks

    c. Replacing traditional safety measures

    d. Reducing the need for project collaboration

PART-TEN

Emerging Trends and Innovations Question

1. What is the primary benefit of using prefabrication and modular construction methods in Missouri construction projects?

    a. Slows down construction timelines

    b. Increases project costs

    c. Accelerates project schedules and reduces on-site work

    d. Eliminates the need for project documentation

2. How does the adoption of Sustainable Building Practices impact general contracting in Missouri?

    a. Increases waste and environmental impact

    b. Reduces energy efficiency

    c. Enhances environmental responsibility and lowers operating costs

    d. Eliminates the need for safety measures

3. What role does 5G technology play in construction projects in Missouri?

    a. Replacing traditional communication methods

    b. Slowing down data transfer rates

    c. Eliminating the need for project collaboration

    d. Increasing project costs

4. How does the use of Augmented Reality (AR) benefit general contractors in Missouri?

    a. Enhancing project communication

    b. Providing real-time data on project costs

    c. Replacing traditional safety measures

    d. Offering visual overlays of project information on the physical site

5. In Missouri, what is the impact of the integration of Artificial Intelligence (AI) in construction management?

   a. Increases project costs

   b. Reduces reliance on data analysis for decision-making

   c. Enhances data-driven decision-making and project optimization

   d. Eliminates the need for project collaboration

6. How does the use of Drones or Unmanned Aerial Vehicles (UAVs) benefit construction projects in Missouri?

   a. Enhancing project communication

   b. Providing real-time project cost analysis

   c. Aiding in site surveys, inspections, and monitoring

   d. Eliminating the need for project collaboration

7. What is the significance of blockchain technology in the construction industry in Missouri?

   a. Slows down project timelines

   b. Increases project costs

   c. Enhances transparency, security, and efficiency in project transactions

   d. Eliminates the need for project collaboration

8. How does the adoption of Building Information Modeling (BIM) impact collaboration in Missouri construction projects?

   a. Increases project costs

   b. Hampers communication among project stakeholders

   c. Enhances collaboration and coordination among project stakeholders

   d. Eliminates the need for project documentation

9. What is the role of robotics in construction projects in Missouri?

    a. Replacing human workers entirely

    b. Increasing the risk of accidents

    c. Automating repetitive and labor-intensive tasks to improve efficiency

    d. Eliminating the need for project collaboration

10. How does the implementation of Internet of Things (IoT) technology benefit construction projects in Missouri?

    a. Increases project costs

    b. Reduces data collection capabilities

    c. Connects and collects data from construction equipment and devices

    d. Eliminates the need for project collaboration

11. What is the impact of 3D printing on construction materials in Missouri?

    a. Increases reliance on traditional construction materials

    b. Decreases design flexibility

    c. Allows for innovative and customized construction materials

    d. Eliminates the need for safety measures

12. How does the use of Smart Construction Equipment improve project efficiency in Missouri?

    a. Increases project costs

    b. Reduces the speed and efficiency of construction tasks

    c. Provides real-time data and diagnostics for construction equipment

    d. Eliminates the need for project documentation

13. What role do collaborative project delivery methods play in emerging trends in Missouri construction?

    a. Increase project costs

    b. Enhance collaboration among project stakeholders

    c. Eliminate the need for project documentation

    d. Shift responsibility to subcontractors

14. How does the use of Autonomous Construction Vehicles impact construction projects in Missouri?

    a. Slows down project timelines

    b. Increases reliance on human-operated vehicles

    c. Automates tasks such as excavation and material handling

    d. Eliminates the need for safety measures

15. In Missouri, what is the significance of the adoption of Lean Construction principles?

    a. Increases waste and inefficiencies

    b. Slows down project timelines

    c. Improves project efficiency and reduces waste

    d. Eliminates the need for safety measures

16. How does the use of Predictive Analytics benefit general contractors in Missouri?

    a. Increases project costs

    b. Reduces the accuracy of project forecasting

    c. Analyzes data to predict project outcomes and optimize decision-making

    d. Eliminates the need for project collaboration

17. What is the impact of Robotics Process Automation (RPA) on administrative tasks in Missouri construction management?

    a. Increases reliance on manual administrative tasks

    b. Slows down administrative processes

    c. Automates routine and repetitive administrative tasks

    d. Eliminates the need for project collaboration

18. How does the integration of Environmental Monitoring Technology contribute to sustainable construction in Missouri?

    a. Increases environmental impact

    b. Slows down project timelines

    c. Monitors and manages environmental impacts, promoting sustainability

    d. Eliminates the need for safety measures

19. What is the significance of the Circular Economy concept in Missouri construction practices?

    a. Promotes a linear approach to resource usage

    b. Increases waste and inefficiencies

    c. Aims to minimize waste and promote the reuse of materials

    d. Eliminates the need for safety measures

20. How does the use of Real-time Project Collaboration Platforms impact project communication in Missouri construction projects?

    a. Slows down communication among project stakeholders

    b. Increases project costs

    c. Enhances real-time communication and collaboration among project team members

    d. Eliminates the need for project documentation

21. What role does Human Augmentation Technology play in improving worker efficiency in Missouri construction projects?

    a. Increases physical strain on workers

    b. Slows down construction tasks

    c. Enhances worker capabilities through technology

    d. Eliminates the need for safety measures

22. How does the implementation of Advanced Surveying Technologies impact accuracy in Missouri construction projects?

    a. Increases inaccuracies in site measurements

    b. Slows down the surveying process

    c. Provides precise and detailed site measurements, improving accuracy

    d. Eliminates the need for safety measures

23. What is the role of Predictive Maintenance in the management of construction equipment in Missouri?

    a. Increases the risk of equipment breakdowns

    b. Slows down equipment maintenance processes

    c. Predicts when equipment maintenance is needed, minimizing downtime

    d. Eliminates the need for safety measures

24. How does the adoption of Green Building Certification impact construction practices in Missouri?

    a. Promotes environmentally harmful construction practices

    b. Slows down project timelines

    c. Encourages sustainable and environmentally friendly construction practices

    d. Eliminates the need for safety measures

25. What is the role of Digital Twins in construction project management in Missouri?

   a. Slows down project timelines

   b. Increases reliance on manual project management processes

   c. Creates a digital replica of the physical construction project for analysis and optimization

   d. Eliminates the need for safety measures

PART-ELEVEN

Common Challenges Faced by General Contractors Question

1. What is a common challenge faced by general contractors in Missouri during the bidding process?

    a. Lack of skilled labor

    b. Inaccurate cost estimation

    c. Delayed project approvals

    d. Limited subcontractor availability

2. How does weather impact construction projects in Missouri, posing a challenge for general contractors?

    a. Increases project efficiency

    b. Causes delays and disruptions

    c. Reduces material costs

    d. Improves worker safety

3. What is a common risk associated with subcontractor relationships for general contractors in Missouri?

    a. Accelerated project timelines

    b. Increased project collaboration

    c. Subcontractor default or non-performance

    d. Streamlined communication

4. How does changing regulatory requirements pose a challenge for general contractors in Missouri?

    a. Simplifies project approvals

    b. Reduces compliance efforts

    c. Increases the risk of legal issues

    d. Enhances project efficiency

5. In Missouri, what is a common issue related to project financing that general contractors may face?

   a. Excess funding availability

   b. Difficulty in securing adequate project financing

   c. Limited budget constraints

   d. Accelerated project timelines

6. How can labor shortages impact general contractors in Missouri?

   a. Improve project efficiency

   b. Accelerate project timelines

   c. Result in increased labor costs and project delays

   d. Streamline communication among workers

7. What role does technology adoption play in the challenges faced by general contractors in Missouri?

   a. Simplifies project management

   b. Eliminates communication barriers

   c. Poses a learning curve and implementation challenges

   d. Reduces the need for skilled labor

8. How does the lack of effective communication impact general contractors in Missouri?

   a. Enhances project collaboration

   b. Reduces the risk of disputes

   c. Leads to misunderstandings and project delays

   d. Accelerates project timelines

9. What is a common challenge related to project scheduling for general contractors in Missouri?

   a. Excess time available for project completion

   b. Inefficient use of resources

   c. Streamlined communication among project stakeholders

   d. Accelerated project timelines

10. How can economic fluctuations impact general contractors in Missouri?

    a. Increase project funding availability

    b. Stabilize material costs

    c. Result in uncertainty, affecting project demand and financing

    d. Simplify budget constraints

11. What is a common challenge associated with safety compliance for general contractors in Missouri?

    a. Reduced need for safety measures

    b. Increased risk of accidents and injuries

    c. Streamlined communication among workers

    d. Accelerated project timelines

12. How does the lack of skilled labor impact project quality for general contractors in Missouri?

    a. Enhances project quality

    b. Results in improved workmanship

    c. Leads to subpar construction quality

    d. Reduces the need for project documentation

13. What is a common challenge associated with project documentation for general contractors in Missouri?

    a. Excess availability of documentation

    b. Insufficient record-keeping and documentation

    c. Streamlined communication among project stakeholders

    d. Accelerated project timelines

14. How does the risk of construction litigation impact general contractors in Missouri?

    a. Reduces the need for legal representation

    b. Increases the risk of legal disputes and associated costs

    c. Accelerates project timelines

    d. Streamlines communication among project stakeholders

15. In Missouri, what is a common challenge related to project scope changes for general contractors?

    a. Stable project scope throughout construction

    b. Difficulty in managing and accommodating frequent scope changes

    c. Accelerated project timelines

    d. Streamlined communication among project stakeholders

16. How can subcontractor performance impact the success of general contractors in Missouri?

    a. Accelerate project timelines

    b. Enhance project collaboration

    c. Pose a risk of delays and quality issues

    d. Streamline communication among workers

17. What is a common challenge associated with project procurement for general contractors in Missouri?

    a. Excess availability of suppliers

    b. Difficulty in sourcing quality materials and services

    c. Accelerated project timelines

    d. Streamlined communication among project stakeholders

18. How does the lack of effective risk management impact general contractors in Missouri?

    a. Reduces the need for risk mitigation strategies

    b. Increases the risk of unforeseen challenges and financial losses

    c. Accelerates project timelines

    d. Streamlines communication among workers

19. What role does community opposition or public resistance play as a challenge for general contractors in Missouri?

    a. Accelerates project timelines

    b. Enhances community collaboration

    c. Poses a risk of project delays and legal hurdles

    d. Reduces the need for project documentation

20. How does the lack of standardized processes impact general contractors in Missouri?

    a. Streamlines project management tasks

    b. Enhances project collaboration

    c. Increases the risk of inefficiencies and errors

    d. Accelerates project timelines

21. What is a common challenge associated with project quality control for general contractors in Missouri?

    a. Excess quality control measures

    b. Difficulty in maintaining consistent quality standards

    c. Accelerated project timelines

    d. Streamlined communication among project stakeholders

22. How can geopolitical factors impact general contractors in Missouri?

    a. Have no effect on construction projects

    b. Increase project funding availability

    c. Introduce uncertainties affecting material costs and project timelines

    d. Accelerate project timelines

23. What is a common challenge associated with subcontractor coordination for general contractors in Missouri?

    a. Smooth coordination with minimal challenges

    b. Difficulty in managing multiple subcontractors and schedules

    c. Accelerated project timelines

    d. Streamlined communication among project stakeholders

24. How does the lack of innovative technologies impact general contractors in Missouri?

    a. Accelerates project timelines

    b. Enhances project collaboration

    c. Increases the risk of falling behind in competitiveness

    d. Streamlines communication among workers

25. In Missouri, what is a common challenge associated with project closeout for general contractors?

    a. Efficient and smooth project closeout processes

    b. Difficulty in resolving outstanding issues and obtaining project sign-off

    c. Accelerated project timelines

    d. Streamlined communication among project stakeholders

PART-TWELEVE

Case Studies Question

1. A general contractor in Missouri faced unexpected delays due to severe weather conditions. What could have been a contributing factor to this delay?

    a. Inefficient project management

    b. Lack of skilled labor

    c. Changing regulatory requirements

    d. Adequate project financing

2. A construction project in Missouri experienced cost overruns. What factor could have led to this issue?

    a. Accurate cost estimation

    b. Timely project approvals

    c. Changing project scope

    d. Effective risk management

3. A general contractor faced legal disputes with subcontractors. What might have contributed to this situation?

    a. Strong subcontractor relationships

    b. Clear communication

    c. Insufficient contract documentation

    d. Adequate project financing

4. A construction project in Missouri struggled with community opposition. What could be a possible cause of this challenge?

   a. Transparent communication

   b. Alignment with community needs

   c. Lack of community engagement

   d. Efficient project management

5. A general contractor faced delays in project approvals. What factor might have caused this delay?

   a. Streamlined communication

   b. Changing regulatory requirements

   c. Timely project financing

   d. Efficient project management

6. A construction project in Missouri struggled with safety compliance issues. What might be a potential cause?

   a. Comprehensive safety training programs

   b. Lack of adherence to safety regulations

   c. Adequate skilled labor

   d. Advanced safety equipment

7. A general contractor faced challenges with subcontractor performance. What could have contributed to this issue?

   a. Efficient subcontractor selection

   b. Clear project communication

   c. Lack of due diligence in subcontractor evaluation

   d. Adequate project financing

8. A construction project in Missouri experienced difficulties in securing project financing. What might have caused this challenge?

    a. Economic stability

    b. Transparent financial documentation

    c. Unstable economic conditions

    d. Accurate project cost estimation

9. A general contractor faced disputes related to project scope changes. What might have caused this issue?

    a. Well-defined project scope

    b. Inefficient project management

    c. Clear communication

    d. Insufficient change order processes

10. A construction project in Missouri struggled with quality control. What could be a potential cause of this challenge?

    a. Skilled labor availability

    b. Consistent quality control measures

    c. Efficient project management

    d. Lack of standardized processes

11. A general contractor faced challenges in community collaboration. What might have contributed to this situation?

    a. Effective community engagement

    b. Transparent communication

    c. Lack of alignment with community needs

    d. Timely project approvals

12. A construction project in Missouri experienced delays due to geopolitical factors. What could be a potential cause?

    a. Stable geopolitical conditions

    b. Unstable political situations

    c. Transparent communication with stakeholders

    d. Efficient project management

13. A general contractor faced challenges in subcontractor coordination. What might have contributed to this issue?

    a. Effective communication with subcontractors

    b. Efficient project management

    c. Lack of standardized processes

    d. Skilled subcontractor availability

14. A construction project in Missouri struggled with innovation adoption. What could be a potential cause of this challenge?

    a. Robust innovation culture

    b. Transparent communication

    c. Lack of awareness and resistance to change

    d. Adequate project financing

15. A general contractor faced difficulties in project closeout. What might have contributed to this challenge?

    a. Efficient resolution of outstanding issues

    b. Timely project approvals

    c. Streamlined communication with stakeholders

    d. Inefficient project management

PART-FOURTEEN

Future Outlook of the Construction Industry Question

1. What is a key driver shaping the future of the construction industry in Missouri?

    a. Decreasing demand for infrastructure projects

    b. Advancements in construction technology

    c. Reduction in skilled labor availability

    d. Reliance on traditional construction methods

2. How does the adoption of sustainable practices impact the future outlook of the construction industry in Missouri?

    a. Increases environmental impact

    b. Slows down project timelines

    c. Enhances long-term viability and resilience

    d. Eliminates the need for safety measures

3. What role does workforce diversity play in the future of the construction industry in Missouri?

    a. Hampers communication among team members

    b. Reduces the need for skilled labor

    c. Fosters innovation and addresses labor shortages

    d. Accelerates project timelines

4. How does the integration of Building Information Modeling (BIM) impact project efficiency in the future of the construction industry in Missouri?

    a. Increases project costs

    b. Slows down collaboration among stakeholders

    c. Enhances project efficiency and coordination

    d. Eliminates the need for project documentation

5. What is the significance of off-site construction methods in the future of construction in Missouri?

    a. Increases reliance on on-site labor

    b. Slows down construction timelines

    c. Improves project efficiency and reduces on-site work

    d. Reduces the need for project collaboration

6. How does the adoption of robotics in construction impact the future workforce in Missouri?

    a. Reduces the need for human labor entirely

    b. Enhances worker safety and efficiency

    c. Increases labor costs

    d. Eliminates the need for skilled workers

7. What role does renewable energy integration play in the future of construction projects in Missouri?

    a. Increases reliance on non-renewable energy sources

    b. Slows down project approvals

    c. Promotes sustainable and energy-efficient construction

    d. Eliminates the need for safety measures

8. How does the use of Augmented Reality (AR) impact project design and visualization in the future of construction in Missouri?

    a. Reduces the need for project visualization

    b. Slows down design processes

    c. Enhances project design and visualization capabilities

    d. Increases project costs

9. What is the impact of 5G technology on communication and collaboration in the future of construction in Missouri?

   a. Slows down data transfer rates
   b. Hampers communication among project stakeholders
   c. Enhances real-time communication and collaboration
   d. Reduces the need for project documentation

10. How does the use of Artificial Intelligence (AI) impact decision-making in the future of construction management in Missouri?

    a. Increases reliance on human decision-making
    b. Reduces the accuracy of project forecasting
    c. Enhances data-driven decision-making and project optimization
    d. Eliminates the need for project collaboration

11. In the future of construction in Missouri, what is the role of prefabrication and modular construction methods?

    a. Slows down project schedules
    b. Increases on-site work and labor requirements
    c. Accelerates project schedules and reduces on-site work
    d. Eliminates the need for project documentation

12. How does the implementation of Internet of Things (IoT) benefit construction projects in the future of the industry in Missouri?

    a. Increases project costs
    b. Reduces data collection capabilities
    c. Connects and collects data from construction equipment and devices
    d. Eliminates the need for project collaboration

13. What is the significance of sustainability certifications like LEED in the future of construction practices in Missouri?

    a. Promotes environmentally harmful construction practices

    b. Slows down project approvals

    c. Encourages sustainable and environmentally friendly construction practices

    d. Eliminates the need for safety measures

14. How does the use of Drones or Unmanned Aerial Vehicles (UAVs) benefit construction projects in the future of the industry in Missouri?

    a. Hampers communication among project stakeholders

    b. Increases project costs

    c. Aids in site surveys, inspections, and monitoring

    d. Eliminates the need for project documentation

15. What is the impact of blockchain technology on project transactions and documentation in the future of construction in Missouri?

    a. Slows down project timelines

    b. Increases project costs

    c. Enhances transparency, security, and efficiency in project transactions

    d. Eliminates the need for project collaboration

16. How does the adoption of 3D printing technology impact construction methods in the future of the industry in Missouri?

    a. Reduces the need for on-site construction

    b. Slows down project timelines

    c. Increases material costs

    d. Eliminates the need for skilled labor

17. What is the significance of a Circular Economy approach in the future of construction practices in Missouri?

    a. Promotes a linear approach to resource usage

    b. Increases waste and inefficiencies

    c. Aims to minimize waste and promote the reuse of materials

    d. Eliminates the need for safety measures

18. How does the future of construction in Missouri address the challenge of skilled labor shortages?

    a. Increased reliance on traditional labor sources

    b. Adoption of workforce development programs and training initiatives

    c. Elimination of the need for skilled labor

    d. Reduction in project timelines

19. What role does resilience planning play in the future of construction projects in Missouri?

    a. Increases vulnerability to unforeseen challenges

    b. Slows down project timelines

    c. Enhances project resilience to natural disasters and external shocks

    d. Eliminates the need for risk management

20. How does the incorporation of smart cities concepts impact the future of urban construction in Missouri?

    a. Hampers communication among city stakeholders

    b. Slows down urban development

    c. Enhances efficiency through interconnected urban infrastructure

    d. Reduces the need for urban planning

21. In the future of construction in Missouri, what is the role of government policies and incentives?

    a. Increase bureaucratic hurdles

    b. Encourage sustainable and innovative construction practices

    c. Slow down project approvals

    d. Eliminate the need for compliance

22. How does the focus on reskilling and upskilling workers impact the future of the construction industry in Missouri?

    a. Increases reliance on traditional skills

    b. Slows down workforce development initiatives

    c. Addresses evolving skill requirements and enhances workforce capabilities

    d. Eliminates the need for workforce training

23. What is the role of digital twins in the future of construction project management in Missouri?

    a. Slows down project timelines

    b. Increases reliance on manual project management processes

    c. Creates a digital replica of the physical construction project for analysis and optimization

    d. Eliminates the need for safety measures

24. How does the implementation of lean construction principles impact the future efficiency of projects in Missouri?

    a. Increases project waste and inefficiencies

    b. Slows down project timelines

    c. Streamlines processes and reduces waste

    d. Eliminates the need for project collaboration

25. What is the impact of global trends and market dynamics on the future competitiveness of the construction industry in Missouri?

    a. Increases isolation from global trends

    b. Enhances local market stability

    c. Introduces uncertainties and requires adaptability

    d. Eliminates the need for market analysis

PART-FIFTEEN

General contractor Mathematics Calculations Question

1. What is the formula for calculating the volume of a rectangular prism?

    a. Volume = length × width × height

    b. Volume = length + width + height

    c. Volume = 2 × (length + width + height)

    d. Volume = length ÷ width ÷ height

2. If a room measures 15 feet in length, 10 feet in width, and 8 feet in height, what is the total cubic footage?

    a. 1,000 cubic feet

    b. 1,200 cubic feet

    c. 1,500 cubic feet

    d. 1,800 cubic feet

3. What is the perimeter of a square with sides measuring 12 feet?

    a. 24 feet

    b. 36 feet

    c. 48 feet

    d. 60 feet

4. If a construction material costs $6 per square foot, what is the total cost of covering a floor that is 20 feet in length and 15 feet in width?

    a. $900

    b. $1,200

    c. $1,500

    d. $1,800

5. What is the percentage decrease if a construction project's budget decreases from $80,000 to $64,000?

    a. 10%

    b. 20%

    c. 25%

    d. 30%

6. A construction project is scheduled to be completed in 15 weeks. If it is already in its 10th week, what percentage of the project is complete?

    a. 30%

    b. 45%

    c. 60%

    d. 75%

7. What is the slope of a roof with a rise of 6 feet and a run of 9 feet?

    a. 0.5

    b. 0.67

    c. 1

    d. 1.5

8. If a construction project requires 25 cubic yards of soil, and each truck can deliver 5 cubic yards, how many trucks are needed?

    a. 3

    b. 4

    c. 5

    d. 6

9. If a construction worker earns $30 per hour and works 50 hours in a week, what is the weekly earnings?

    a. $1,000

    b. $1,200

    c. $1,400

    d. $1,500

10. What is the square root of 169?

    a. 10

    b. 11

    c. 12

    d. 13

11. If the cost of materials for a project is $10,000 and the labor cost is $15,000, what is the total project cost?

    a. $20,000

    b. $25,000

    c. $30,000

    d. $35,000

12. If a construction project is budgeted for 600 labor hours, and 480 hours have been worked, what percentage of the project is complete?

    a. 60%

    b. 70%

    c. 80%

    d. 90%

13. What is the area of a triangular-shaped construction site with a base of 15 feet and a height of 9 feet?

    a. 45 square feet

    b. 67.5 square feet

    c. 90 square feet

    d. 112.5 square feet

14. If the scale on a construction blueprint is 1:75, what does it mean?

    a. 1 inch on the blueprint represents 75 inches in reality

    b. 1 foot on the blueprint represents 75 feet in reality

    c. 1 unit on the blueprint represents 75 units in reality

    d. 1 meter on the blueprint represents 75 meters in reality

15. If a construction project requires 30 cubic yards of concrete, and each truck can deliver 6 cubic yards, how many trucks are needed?

    a. 3

    b. 4

    c. 5

    d. 6

16. What is the perimeter of a right-angled triangle with sides measuring 8, 15, and 17 units?

    a. 33 units

    b. 40 units

    c. 42 units

    d. 50 units

17. If a construction project is delayed by 3 weeks, and the original timeline was 12 weeks, what is the percentage increase in the project duration?

    a. 15%

    b. 20%

    c. 25%

    d. 30%

18. What is the formula for calculating the circumference of a circle?

    a. Circumference = π × diameter

    b. Circumference = 2 × π × radius

    c. Circumference = π × radius²

    d. Circumference = 2 × π × diameter

19. If a construction project requires 20 tons of gravel, and each truck can carry 4 tons, how many trucks are needed?

    a. 3

    b. 4

    c. 5

    d. 6

20. What is the slope of a line that passes through the points (3, 6) and (5, 10)?

    a. 2

    b. 3

    c. 4

    d. 5

21. If a construction project requires pouring concrete for a slab with dimensions 25 feet by 35 feet and a depth of 8 inches, what is the volume of concrete needed in cubic yards?

    a. 16.67

    b. 18.75

    c. 20

    d. 22.22

22. What is the formula for calculating the area of a circle?

    a. Area = π × diameter

    b. Area = 2 × π × radius

    c. Area = π × radius²

    d. Area = 2 × π × diameter

23. If a construction project requires 25 gallons of paint, and each gallon can cover 150 square feet, how many square feet can be painted with 8 gallons?

    a. 900

    b. 1,000

    c. 1,200

    d. 1,500

24. What is the Pythagorean Theorem used for in construction calculations?

    a. Calculating the area of a triangle

    b. Finding the perimeter of a rectangle

    c. Determining the hypotenuse of a right-angled triangle

    d. Measuring the circumference of a circle

25. If a construction project requires 50 sheets of plywood, and each sheet measures 4 feet by 8 feet, what is the total square footage of plywood needed?

    a. 1,200 square feet

    b. 1,600 square feet

    c. 2,000 square feet

    d. 2,400 square feet

26. What is the formula for calculating the area of a rectangular room in square feet?

    a. Length × Width

    b. Length ÷ Width

    c. (Length + Width) ÷ 2

    d. Length + Width

27. In construction, what does the term "linear feet" refer to?

    a. Square footage of a room

    b. Measurement of volume

    c. Measurement of length

    d. Thickness of materials

28. What is the formula for calculating the volume of a rectangular prism or a cuboid?

    a. Length × Width × Height

    b. (Length + Width) × Height

    c. Length ÷ Width ÷ Height

    d. Length × Width + Height

29. When calculating the area of a circle, what is the constant used for the mathematical formula?

    a. π (pi)

    b. e (Euler's number)

    c. √2 (square root of 2)

    d. φ (phi)

30. What is the Pythagorean Theorem used for in construction calculations?

    a. Calculating areas of irregular shapes

    b. Finding the volume of a cylinder

    c. Determining angles in right-angled triangles

    d. Measuring linear feet

31. In construction, how is the slope of a roof expressed mathematically?

    a. Rise/Run

    b. Rise × Run

    c. Rise - Run

    d. Run/Rise

32. What is the purpose of the calculation for "cut and fill" in site grading?

    a. Calculating material costs

    b. Determining the volume of soil to be removed or added

    c. Estimating labor hours

    d. Measuring linear feet

33. How is the area of an irregular shape calculated when using the trapezoidal rule?

    a. (Base1 + Base2) × Height ÷ 2

    b. Base1 × Base2 × Height

    c. Base1 × Height + Base2

    d. (Base1 - Base2) × Height ÷ 2

34. What is the formula for calculating the volume of a cylinder?

    a. $\pi r^2 h$

    b. $2\pi r h$

    c. $\pi r + h$

    d. $(\pi r + h) \div 2$

35. In construction cost estimation, what does the term "unit rate" refer to?

    a. The total project cost

    b. The cost per square foot

    c. The cost per linear foot

    d. The hourly labor rate

36. What is the formula for calculating the perimeter of a rectangle?

    a. 2 × (Length + Width)

    b. Length × Width

    c. Length + Width

    d. 2 × Length + 2 × Width

37. When calculating concrete volume for a circular column, what is the formula used?

    a. $\pi r^2 h$

    b. $2\pi r h$

    c. $(\pi r + h) \div 2$

    d. $(2\pi r + h) \div 2$

38. What is the purpose of calculating the "net present value" (NPV) in financial analysis for construction projects?

    a. Estimating labor costs

    b. Evaluating the project's profitability over time

    c. Determining concrete strength

    d. Measuring linear feet

39. How is the surface area of a cylinder calculated?

    a. $2\pi r$

    b. $2\pi r^2 + 2\pi r h$

    c. $\pi r + h$

    d. $2\pi r h$

40. In construction project scheduling, what does the critical path represent?

    a. The shortest path to completion

    b. The longest path to completion

    c. The path with the fewest tasks

    d. The path with the most tasks

41. What does the term "percent slope" represent in construction calculations?

    a. The angle of inclination

    b. The length of a slope

    c. The width of a slope

    d. The cost of materials

42. When calculating the area of a triangle, what is the formula used?

    a. Base × Height

    b. (Base × Height) ÷ 2

    c. Base + Height

    d. Base - Height

43. What is the purpose of calculating the "moment of inertia" in structural engineering?

    a. Estimating labor costs

    b. Determining concrete strength

    c. Evaluating a structure's resistance to bending

    d. Measuring linear feet

44. How is the cost of concrete calculated based on volume and unit price?

    a. Volume × Unit Price

    b. Volume ÷ Unit Price

    c. Unit Price ÷ Volume

    d. Volume + Unit Price

45. What is the formula for calculating the total cost of labor on a construction project?

    a. Hours × Rate

    b. Hours ÷ Rate

    c. Rate ÷ Hours

    d. Hours + Rate

46. How is the aspect ratio of a rectangular shape calculated?

    a. Length ÷ Width

    b. Width ÷ Length

    c. Length × Width

    d. (Length + Width) ÷ 2

47. In construction, what is the purpose of the "pitch" calculation for a roof?

    a. Measuring linear feet

    b. Determining roof slope

    c. Calculating concrete strength

    d. Estimating labor costs

48. What is the formula for calculating the area of a trapezoid?

    a. (Base1 + Base2) ÷ 2 × Height

    b. Base1 × Base2 × Height

    c. (Base1 - Base2) ÷ 2 × Height

    d. Base1 + Base2 + Height

49. How is the cost of materials calculated based on quantity and unit price?

    a. Quantity + Unit Price

    b. Quantity × Unit Price

    c. Unit Price ÷ Quantity

    d. Quantity ÷ Unit Price

50. What is the formula for calculating the load-bearing capacity of a beam in structural engineering?

   a. Load ÷ Area

   b. Area ÷ Load

   c. Load × Area

   d. Load - Area

PART-ONE

Introduction to General Contractors Answer

1. Answer: c) 2,000 square feet

    Explanation: The total square footage is calculated as the quantity of sheets multiplied by the area of each sheet, so 50 sheets × (4 feet × 8 feet) = 2,000 square feet.

2. Answer: a) 18 years

    Explanation: In Missouri, the minimum age requirement for obtaining a general contractor's license is 18 years.

3. Answer: b) Every two years

    Explanation: General contractors in Missouri are required to renew their licenses every two years.

4. Answer: b) Liability insurance

    Explanation: General contractors in Missouri are often required to have liability insurance to cover potential damages.

5. Answer: c) Completion of a qualifying examination

    Explanation: To obtain a general contractor's license in Missouri, candidates typically need to pass a qualifying examination.

6. Answer: b) Fine

    Explanation: Contracting without a license in Missouri can result in fines.

7. Answer: c) To regulate and license contractors

   Explanation: The Missouri Contractor's License Board is responsible for regulating and licensing contractors in the state.

8. Answer: b) Construction contract

   Explanation: A construction contract outlines the terms and conditions of a construction project and is often required for obtaining a building permit.

9. Answer: b) To guarantee the contractor's performance

   Explanation: A bid bond is a guarantee that the contractor will fulfill the terms of a bid if selected for the project.

10. Answer: c) Missouri Department of Labor

    Explanation: The Missouri Department of Labor oversees workplace safety regulations for construction projects in the state.

11. Answer: a) Business license

    Explanation: Subcontractors working on public projects in Missouri often need to have a valid business license.

12. Answer: c) Both residential and commercial projects

    Explanation: A general contractor's license in Missouri is typically required for both residential and commercial projects.

13. Answer: c) Obtaining a surety bond

    Explanation: General contractors in Missouri can demonstrate financial responsibility by obtaining a surety bond.

14. Answer: b) To protect subcontractors' rights to payment

    Explanation: The Missouri Mechanic's Lien Law is designed to protect subcontractors' rights to payment for their work.

15. Answer: a) To determine eligibility for government contracts

    Explanation: The pre-qualification process in Missouri is often used to determine a contractor's eligibility for government contracts.

16. Answer: a) Local municipalities

    Explanation: Building permits are typically issued by local municipalities in Missouri.

17. Answer: c) To provide recourse for unpaid contractors and suppliers

    Explanation: The Missouri Construction Lien Law provides a legal recourse for contractors and suppliers who have not been paid for their work.

18. Answer: c) Passage of a criminal background check

    Explanation: Many licensing authorities, including in Missouri, require general contractor applicants to pass a criminal background check.

19. Answer: b) To ensure fair wages for workers on public construction projects

    Explanation: The Missouri Minimum Wage Law for public works projects aims to ensure fair wages for workers involved in such projects.

20. Answer: c) Associated General Contractors (AGC) of Missouri

    Explanation: The Associated General Contractors (AGC) of Missouri is an organization that provides resources and support for continuing education for contractors.

21. Answer: d) Certification as a Minority Business Enterprise (MBE)

    Explanation: Subcontractors working on state-funded projects in Missouri may be required to be certified as Minority Business Enterprises (MBE) for certain projects.

22. Answer: b) Fine

    Explanation: Violating building codes in Missouri can result in fines.

23. Answer: c) To ensure fair wages for workers on public construction projects

    Explanation: The Prevailing Wage Law in Missouri aims to ensure fair wages for workers on public construction projects.

24. Answer: c) To provide licensing for contractors

    Explanation: The Missouri Division of Professional Registration is responsible for providing licensing for various professions, including contractors.

25. Answer: c) Obtaining bid security

    Explanation: Obtaining bid security is an essential step in the construction bidding process in Missouri, often in the form of a bid bond or other financial guarantee.**

PART-TWO

Qualifications and Skills Answer

1. Answer: c) 5 years

   Explanation: In Missouri, a general contractor typically needs a minimum of 5 years of relevant experience to qualify for a license.

2. Answer: b) Business Administration

   Explanation: While not always required, a degree in Business Administration can be beneficial for a general contractor in Missouri, providing knowledge in management and finance.

3. Answer: b) Project Management Professional (PMP)

   Explanation: A Project Management Professional (PMP) certification can enhance a general contractor's qualifications by demonstrating proficiency in project management.

4. Answer: b) It allows them to perform electrical work

   Explanation: Being a licensed master electrician in Missouri allows a general contractor to perform electrical work without hiring a separate electrician.

5. Answer: c) Conflict resolution

   Explanation: Conflict resolution is a crucial skill for general contractors in Missouri, helping to manage disputes and maintain project momentum.

6. Answer: b) Associated General Contractors (AGC) of Missouri

   Explanation: The Associated General Contractors (AGC) of Missouri is an organization that provides professional development resources for general contractors.

7. Answer: b) To work on projects involving lead-based paint

   Explanation: A Lead-Based Paint Renovation License in Missouri is required for contractors working on projects involving lead-based paint.

8. Answer: c) Clear and concise communication

   Explanation: Clear and concise communication is essential for general contractors in Missouri to ensure that project requirements are understood by all stakeholders.

9. Answer: c) Ensuring compliance with safety regulations

   Explanation: A Safety Coordinator in a general contractor's team is responsible for ensuring compliance with safety regulations on construction sites in Missouri.

10. Answer: c) It facilitates effective subcontractor agreements

    Explanation: Strong negotiation skills are crucial for general contractors in Missouri to establish favorable subcontractor agreements and manage project costs effectively.

11. Answer: b) Holding a surety bond

    Explanation: Being "bonded" in Missouri typically means that a general contractor holds a surety bond, providing financial protection for clients and subcontractors.

12. Answer: c) Highlighting completed projects and capabilities

    Explanation: A general contractor's portfolio in Missouri is used to showcase completed projects and demonstrate their capabilities to potential clients.

13. Answer: b) Overseeing day-to-day operations

    Explanation: The General Superintendent is responsible for overseeing day-to-day operations on a construction project in Missouri.

14. Answer: b) Increased energy efficiency

    Explanation: Knowledge of sustainable construction practices in Missouri can lead to increased energy efficiency in projects, aligning with environmental considerations.

15. Answer: c) Overseeing the quality of work

    Explanation: A Quality Control Manager is responsible for ensuring that the work on a construction project in Missouri meets established quality standards.

16. Answer: a) Attend professional development workshops

    Explanation: Attending professional development workshops is a proactive way for general contractors in Missouri to stay updated on changes in building codes and regulations.

17. Answer: c) Cost estimation

    Explanation: Cost estimation is a crucial skill for general contractors in Missouri to successfully manage budgets and control project costs.

18. Answer: a) To avoid legal liabilities

    Explanation: Knowledge of construction contracts is important for general contractors in Missouri to avoid legal liabilities and ensure compliance with project terms.

19. Answer: b) Providing guidelines for employee safety

    Explanation: A Safety Manual for a general contractor in Missouri provides guidelines and procedures to ensure employee safety on construction sites.

20. Answer: d) Reducing risks associated with subcontractor performance

    Explanation: A comprehensive Subcontractor Qualification Process in Missouri helps general contractors reduce risks associated with subcontractor performance by evaluating their capabilities and qualifications.

21. Answer: c) Participating in community outreach programs

    Explanation: Participating in community outreach programs is a way for general contractors in Missouri to demonstrate a commitment to diversity and inclusion in their projects.

22. Answer: b) Driving construction vehicles on public roads

    Explanation: A Commercial Driver's License (CDL) is required for general contractors in Missouri who need to drive construction vehicles on public roads.

23. Answer: c) Participating in leadership training programs

    Explanation: Participating in leadership training programs is a proactive way for general contractors in Missouri to enhance their leadership skills.

24. Answer: c) Ensuring accessibility in construction projects

    Explanation: Knowledge of the Americans with Disabilities Act (ADA) is important for general contractors in Missouri to ensure accessibility in construction projects and compliance with regulations.

25. Answer: c) Attending industry conferences and seminars

    Explanation: Attending industry conferences and seminars is a proactive way for general contractors in Missouri to stay informed about emerging construction technologies and advancements.**

PART-THREE

Types of Construction Projects Answer

1. Answer: c) Residential construction

   Explanation: Residential construction involves the building of homes, apartments, or condominiums for private occupancy.

2. Answer: b) Civil construction

   Explanation: Civil construction involves projects related to infrastructure development, such as roads, bridges, and utilities.

3. Answer: a) Institutional construction

   Explanation: Institutional construction involves the construction of facilities for healthcare, education, or government purposes.

4. Answer: a) Industrial construction

   Explanation: Industrial construction involves projects related to manufacturing facilities, warehouses, and distribution centers.

5. Answer: c) Commercial construction

   Explanation: Commercial construction involves projects related to retail spaces, office buildings, and shopping centers.

6. Answer: d) Retrofit construction

   Explanation: Retrofit construction in Missouri involves the renovation or expansion of existing structures.

7. Answer: a) Sustainable construction

   Explanation: Sustainable construction involves the use of environmentally friendly materials and practices to reduce the project's impact on the environment.

8. Answer: a) Modular construction

   Explanation: Modular construction involves off-site manufacturing and assembly of building components before being transported to the construction site.

9. Answer: a) Design-Build construction

   Explanation: Design-Build construction involves the simultaneous design and construction phases, allowing for a faster project delivery.

10. Answer: b) Brownfield construction

    Explanation: Brownfield construction in Missouri involves the redevelopment of previously used industrial or commercial sites.

11. Answer: c) High-rise construction

    Explanation: High-rise construction involves the construction of tall buildings, such as skyscrapers.

12. Answer: a) Mass timber construction

    Explanation: Mass timber construction involves the use of large, solid wood panels for building construction.

13. Answer: c) Civil construction

    Explanation: Civil construction in Missouri might involve the construction of highways, bridges, and tunnels.

14. Answer: c) Recreational construction

   Explanation: Recreational construction involves the construction of facilities for entertainment, such as theaters, stadiums, and amusement parks.

15. Answer: b) Subterranean construction

   Explanation: Subterranean construction involves the construction of structures below the ground surface.

16. Answer: a) Religious construction

   Explanation: Religious construction involves the construction of structures for religious purposes, such as churches, mosques, and temples.

17. Answer: b) Preservation construction

   Explanation: Preservation construction in Missouri might involve the restoration of historic buildings or landmarks.

18. Answer: a) Laboratory construction

   Explanation: Laboratory construction involves the construction of facilities for research, development, and scientific purposes.

19. Answer: c) Warehousing construction

   Explanation: Warehousing construction involves the construction of structures for the storage of goods, such as warehouses and distribution centers.

20. Answer: b) Manufacturing construction

   Explanation: Manufacturing construction involves the creation of specialized spaces for the production of goods or manufacturing processes.

21. Answer: c) Recreation construction

    Explanation: Recreation construction in Missouri might involve the construction of public parks, sports fields, or playgrounds.

22. Answer: a) Cultural construction

    Explanation: Cultural construction involves the construction of facilities for the arts, such as museums, galleries, and theaters.

23. Answer: a) Educational construction

    Explanation: Educational construction involves the construction of structures for educational purposes, such as schools and universities.

24. Answer: d) Water and wastewater construction

    Explanation: Water and wastewater construction involves the construction of structures for the storage and treatment of water and wastewater.

25. Answer: a) Hospitality construction

    Explanation: Hospitality construction in Missouri might involve the construction of facilities for the hospitality industry, such as hotels and resorts.**

PART-FOUR

Responsibilities of General Contractors Answer

1. Answer: b) Managing construction projects

   Explanation: General contractors are primarily responsible for overseeing and managing construction projects.

2. Answer: c) Missouri Division of Professional Registration

   Explanation: The Missouri Division of Professional Registration is responsible for issuing licenses to general contractors.

3. Answer: a) Passing a written exam

   Explanation: Many states, including Missouri, require general contractors to pass a written exam to obtain a license.

4. Answer: d) Providing medical services to workers

   Explanation: General contractors are not responsible for providing medical services to workers; that is usually the role of health professionals.

5. Answer: c) Construction contract

   Explanation: A construction contract is a legal document that outlines the terms and conditions of a construction project and is signed by both parties involved.

6. Answer: c) Guaranteeing completion of the project

   Explanation: A performance bond provides a guarantee that the project will be completed as per the terms of the contract.

7. Answer: c) Department of Labor and Industrial Relations

   Explanation: The Department of Labor and Industrial Relations in Missouri is typically responsible for enforcing building codes.

8. Answer: b) Providing personal protective equipment (PPE)

   Explanation: General contractors are responsible for providing PPE to ensure the safety of workers on a construction site.

9. Answer: c) Builder's risk insurance

   Explanation: Builder's risk insurance is a common type of insurance coverage for general contractors, covering damage to the construction project during construction.

10. Answer: b) Timely payment to subcontractors

    Explanation: The Missouri Prompt Pay Act addresses the timely payment of subcontractors by general contractors.

11. Answer: b) Releases the right to file a mechanics lien

    Explanation: A lien waiver releases the right of a contractor or subcontractor to file a mechanics lien against the property.

12. Answer: c) Missouri Division of Workforce Development

    Explanation: The Missouri Division of Workforce Development oversees apprenticeship programs in the state.

13. Answer: a) Every 2 years

    Explanation: General contractors in Missouri typically need to renew their licenses every two years.

14. Answer: a) Establishing minimum wages for construction workers

    Explanation: The Prevailing Wage law establishes minimum wages for construction workers on public works projects in Missouri.

15. Answer: b) Communicating with local authorities

    Explanation: General contractors are typically responsible for communicating with local authorities and obtaining necessary permits for a construction project.

16. Answer: b) It limits the time frame for filing construction defect claims

    Explanation: The Right to Repair Act often limits the time frame within which construction defect claims can be filed.

17. Answer: c) Confirming insurance coverage

    Explanation: A certificate of insurance confirms that a general contractor has the necessary insurance coverage.

18. Answer: d) Environmental impact statement

    Explanation: Environmental impact statements are typically not part of the standard bidding process for construction projects.

19. Answer: b) Giving preference to local contractors

    Explanation: The Missouri Contractors' Preference Law aims to give preference to local contractors in certain situations.

20. Answer: a) Department of Insurance, Financial Institutions & Professional Registration

    Explanation: The Department of Insurance, Financial Institutions & Professional Registration often handles workers' compensation claims.

21. Answer: b) A certificate of occupancy

    Explanation: A "Substantial Completion" certificate is a document declaring that the construction project is essentially complete and can be occupied or used.

22. Answer: c) It ensures transparency in government-related activities

    Explanation: The Missouri Sunshine Law promotes transparency in government activities, which may impact general contractors involved in public projects.

23. Answer: b) Modifying the construction contract terms

    Explanation: A change order is a document that modifies the terms of the construction contract, often due to changes in project scope or conditions.

24. Answer: a) Arbitrating conflicts between subcontractors

    Explanation: General contractors may play a role in resolving disputes, often through methods like arbitration, between subcontractors or parties involved in the construction project.

25. Answer: c) Communicating clearly with all parties

    Explanation: Clear communication with all parties involved in a construction project can help prevent misunderstandings and legal disputes.

PART-FIVE

Project Phases and General Contractor Involvement Answer

1. Answer: b) Design Phase

   Explanation: General contractors often become involved during the Design Phase to provide input on constructability, budgeting, and scheduling.

2. Answer: c) Establishing project objectives and parameters

   Explanation: The Pre-Construction Phase focuses on defining project goals, setting parameters, and planning before actual construction begins.

3. Answer: c) Project management plan

   Explanation: The Project Management Plan outlines the project scope, schedule, and budget during the Pre-Construction Phase.

4. Answer: b) Providing input on constructability and costs

   Explanation: During the Design Phase, general contractors provide valuable input on constructability, costs, and logistics.

5. Answer: a) Inviting contractors to submit bids

   Explanation: The Request for Proposal (RFP) invites contractors to submit their bids for the construction project.

6. Answer: d) Construction Phase

   Explanation: The Construction Phase involves the actual physical construction of the project.

7. Answer: a) Authorizing construction to begin

   Explanation: A Notice to Proceed authorizes the general contractor to start construction activities.

8. Answer: b) Managing the construction process

   Explanation: The general contractor is responsible for managing and overseeing the construction process during this phase.

9. Answer: b) Construction contract

   Explanation: The Construction Contract outlines the terms, conditions, and responsibilities of the parties involved in the construction project.

10. Answer: b) Modifying the construction contract terms

    Explanation: A Change Order is a document that modifies the terms of the construction contract, often due to changes in project scope or conditions.

11. Answer: c) Completing punch lists and inspections

    Explanation: The Post-Construction Phase focuses on completing punch lists, final inspections, and closing out the project.

12. Answer: b) Certificate of Substantial Completion

    Explanation: The Certificate of Substantial Completion signifies the completion of the construction project and the owner's acceptance of the work.

13. Answer: b) Confirming the completion of all project work

    Explanation: The Final Completion Certificate confirms the completion of all project work and signifies the end of the project.

14. Answer: b) Extending project warranties

   Explanation: During the Warranty Phase, the general contractor may address warranty issues and ensure that any necessary repairs are made.

15. Answer: b) It withholds a portion of payments until project completion

   Explanation: Retention involves withholding a portion of payments until the project is completed to ensure that subcontractors fulfill their obligations.

16. Answer: c) A list of incomplete or deficient work

   Explanation: A Punch List identifies incomplete or deficient work that needs to be addressed before project completion.

17. Answer: b) Certifying completion of the project

   Explanation: The Certificate of Occupancy certifies that the construction project complies with building codes and is suitable for occupancy.

18. Answer: b) Completing punch lists and inspections

   Explanation: The Closeout Phase involves completing punch lists, inspections, and other activities to finalize the project.

19. Answer: b) Documenting changes made during construction

   Explanation: As-Built Drawings document changes made during construction and provide an accurate representation of the final project.

20. Answer: c) Finalizing contractual obligations

   Explanation: Project Closeout involves finalizing contractual obligations, completing documentation, and concluding the project.

21. Answer: b) It withholds a portion of payments until project completion

    Explanation: Retention involves withholding a portion of payments until the project is completed to ensure that the general contractor fulfills their obligations.

22. Answer: c) Discussing project objectives and expectations

    Explanation: A Project Kickoff Meeting is held to discuss project objectives, expectations, and the roles of various stakeholders.

23. Answer: a) It ensures timely payment to subcontractors

    Explanation: Pay Applications ensure that subcontractors receive timely payments for completed work.

24. Answer: b) Communicating with local authorities

    Explanation: General contractors are typically responsible for communicating with local authorities and obtaining necessary permits for a construction project.

25. Answer: b) Testing and verifying systems for proper functionality

    Explanation: The Commissioning process involves testing and verifying systems to ensure they function correctly before project completion.

PART-SIX

Building Codes and Regulations Answer

1. Answer: d) Local municipalities and counties

   Explanation: Building codes in Missouri are typically adopted and enforced at the local level by municipalities and counties.

2. Answer: c) To ensure public safety and welfare

   Explanation: The primary purpose of building codes is to ensure public safety and welfare by regulating construction practices.

3. Answer: c) Building codes

   Explanation: Building codes in Missouri contain specific requirements for the construction and design of buildings.

4. Answer: b) Every 5 years

   Explanation: Building codes in Missouri are often updated every five years to incorporate advancements in construction and safety standards.

5. Answer: d) To ensure compliance with building codes

   Explanation: A building permit is issued to ensure that construction activities comply with the relevant building codes.

6. Answer: d) Adding a room to an existing home

   Explanation: Significant alterations, such as adding a room, often require a building permit in Missouri.

7. Answer: c) Fines and penalties

   Explanation: Proceeding without required permits in Missouri may result in fines and penalties.

8. Answer: d) Various inspections throughout the construction process

   Explanation: Different inspections are conducted at various phases of construction to ensure compliance with building codes.

9. Answer: b) A waiver from specific code requirements

   Explanation: A variance in Missouri is a waiver from specific code requirements, granted under certain conditions.

10. Answer: c) Local board of appeals or zoning board

    Explanation: Variances from building code requirements are typically granted by local boards of appeals or zoning boards in Missouri.

11. Answer: c) It mandates accessibility standards

    Explanation: The ADA mandates accessibility standards that may influence building codes in Missouri to ensure inclusivity.

12. Answer: c) Obtaining building permits

    Explanation: General contractors play a role in obtaining necessary building permits to ensure compliance with building codes.

13. Answer: b) Certifying completion of the project

    Explanation: The Certificate of Occupancy certifies that the construction project complies with building codes and is suitable for occupancy.

14. Answer: b) Structural and fire safety

   Explanation: The International Building Code (IBC) primarily addresses structural and fire safety standards.

15. Answer: c) Ensuring energy-efficient building practices

   Explanation: The Energy Conservation Code in Missouri aims to ensure energy-efficient building practices.

16. Answer: c) It addresses fire prevention and safety measures

   Explanation: The Missouri State Fire Code focuses on fire prevention and safety measures in construction projects.

17. Answer: c) Mandating accessibility standards

   Explanation: The Missouri Accessibility Code mandates accessibility standards to ensure inclusivity in construction projects.

18. Answer: d) It establishes criteria for plumbing installations

   Explanation: The International Plumbing Code (IPC) sets standards for plumbing installations in construction projects.

19. Answer: c) Addressing lead-based paint hazards

   Explanation: The Missouri Lead Abatement Code addresses lead-based paint hazards in construction projects.

20. Answer: d) It establishes criteria for mechanical installations

   Explanation: The International Mechanical Code (IMC) sets standards for mechanical installations in construction projects.

21. Answer: b) Immediately correcting violations

    Explanation: General contractors are typically responsible for promptly correcting building code violations on a construction site.

22. Answer: c) It addresses structural safety in buildings

    Explanation: The Missouri Structural Code addresses structural safety standards in buildings.

23. Answer: d) Establishing criteria for fuel gas installations

    Explanation: The International Fuel Gas Code (IFGC) sets standards for fuel gas installations in construction projects.

24. Answer: c) Attending code training sessions and seminars

    Explanation: General contractors can stay informed about code updates by attending training sessions and seminars.

25. Answer: d) It establishes criteria for plumbing installations

    Explanation: The Uniform Plumbing Code (UPC) sets standards for plumbing installations in construction projects.

PART-SEVEN

Contracting and Subcontracting Answer

1. Answer: b) Construction contract

   Explanation: A construction contract is a legal document that outlines the terms and conditions of a construction project and is signed by both parties involved.

2. Answer: c) Inviting contractors to submit bids

   Explanation: A bid proposal is a document that invites contractors to submit their bids for a construction project.

3. Answer: b) Cost-plus contract

   Explanation: In a cost-plus contract, the general contractor is compensated based on a percentage of the total project cost, including overhead and profit.

4. Answer: a) Guaranteed maximum price

   Explanation: A lump sum contract provides a guaranteed maximum price for the project, offering cost certainty to the owner.

5. Answer: b) Guaranteeing completion of the project

   Explanation: A performance bond provides a guarantee that the general contractor will complete the project according to the terms of the contract.

6. Answer: b) Requires prompt payment to subcontractors

    Explanation: The Missouri Prompt Pay Act requires prompt payment to subcontractors and sets guidelines for payment practices in construction contracts.

7. Answer: b) Releases the right to file a mechanics lien

    Explanation: A lien waiver releases the right of a contractor or subcontractor to file a mechanics lien against the property.

8. Answer: c) Withholds a portion of payments until project completion

    Explanation: A retainage clause allows the owner to withhold a portion of payments until the project is completed to ensure that the contractor fulfills their obligations.

9. Answer: b) Cost-plus contract

    Explanation: In a cost-plus contract, the general contractor is compensated based on actual costs plus a fixed fee for profit and overhead.

10. Answer: b) Protecting general contractors from defaulting subcontractors

    Explanation: Subcontractor Default Insurance (SDI) protects general contractors from financial losses in the event of subcontractor default.

11. Answer: b) Gives preference to local subcontractors

    Explanation: The Missouri Contractors' Preference Law gives preference to local subcontractors in certain situations.

12. Answer: c) Hiring and coordinating subcontractors

    Explanation: General contractors are responsible for hiring and coordinating subcontractors for various aspects of a construction project.

13. Answer: d) Passing a pre-qualification process

   Explanation: Subcontractors may need to pass a pre-qualification process to participate in public construction projects in Missouri.

14. Answer: a) Guaranteeing performance of the project

   Explanation: A bid bond guarantees that the contractor will enter into a contract and perform the work if awarded the project.

15. Answer: c) It ensures transparency in government-related activities

   Explanation: The Missouri Sunshine Law promotes transparency in government-related activities, which may impact subcontracting in public projects.

16. Answer: b) Challenging the awarding of a contract

   Explanation: The Bid Protest process allows bidders to challenge the awarding of a contract based on concerns or disputes.

17. Answer: b) Provides financial incentives for minority-owned subcontractors

   Explanation: The Missouri MBE Program provides financial incentives and opportunities for minority-owned businesses in subcontracting.

18. Answer: a) Authorizing construction to begin

   Explanation: The Notice to Proceed authorizes subcontractors to commence their work on a construction project.

19. Answer: c) Complying with safety regulations and guidelines

   Explanation: Subcontractors are responsible for complying with safety regulations and guidelines on the construction site.

20. Answer: b) Withholds a portion of payments until project completion

    Explanation: Retention involves withholding a portion of payments to subcontractors until the project is completed.

21. Answer: c) Establishing the terms between the general contractor and subcontractor

    Explanation: A Subcontractor Agreement outlines the terms and conditions between the general contractor and subcontractor.

22. Answer: d) Filing a mechanics lien

    Explanation: Filing a mechanics lien is a legal remedy for subcontractors to protect themselves from non-payment issues.

23. Answer: c) Guaranteeing performance of subcontracted work

    Explanation: A Subcontractor Performance Bond guarantees the performance of the subcontractor's work on a construction project.

24. Answer: b) Provides protection against default by subcontractors

    Explanation: SDI provides protection for general contractors against financial losses in the event of subcontractor default.

25. Answer: b) Arbitrating conflicts between subcontractors

    Explanation: General contractors may play a role in resolving disputes, often through methods like arbitration, between subcontractors on a construction project.

PART-EIGHT

Risk Management and Insurance Answer

1. Answer: c) Providing coverage for bodily injury or property damage claims

    Explanation: Liability insurance provides coverage for claims related to bodily injury or property damage, protecting the general contractor.

2. Answer: b) Builder's risk insurance

    Explanation: Builder's risk insurance protects against financial losses caused by project delays or interruptions, such as damage to the construction site.

3. Answer: b) Providing coverage for bodily injury to employees

    Explanation: Workers' compensation insurance provides coverage for bodily injury or illness suffered by employees during work.

4. Answer: c) Providing coverage for design errors or negligence

    Explanation: Professional liability insurance provides coverage for claims related to design errors or negligence in the professional services provided.

5. Answer: c) Implementing a Subcontractor Default Insurance (SDI) program

    Explanation: SDI programs can help mitigate the financial risk associated with subcontractor default.

6. Answer: d) Guaranteeing performance of contractual obligations

    Explanation: Surety bonds guarantee the general contractor's performance of contractual obligations to the project owner.

7. Answer: b) Shifts liability to subcontractors

   Explanation: Indemnification clauses can shift liability from the general contractor to subcontractors, reducing the contractor's risk exposure.

8. Answer: c) Providing proof of insurance coverage from subcontractors

   Explanation: A Certificate of Insurance provides proof that subcontractors have the required insurance coverage.

9. Answer: b) Reduces the risk of accidents and injuries

   Explanation: A comprehensive safety program can help reduce the risk of accidents and injuries, improving overall risk management.

10. Answer: d) Allocating certain risks to another party

    Explanation: Hold harmless clauses allocate specific risks and liabilities to another party, providing a form of risk transfer.

11. Answer: d) Assesses the financial stability and capability of subcontractors

    Explanation: Subcontractor prequalification involves assessing the financial stability and capability of subcontractors, reducing the risk of default.

12. Answer: b) Provides discounts on insurance premiums

    Explanation: SHARP recognition may lead to discounts on insurance premiums for general contractors with strong safety and health programs.

13. Answer: d) Sharing the financial responsibility with the insurance company

    Explanation: An insurance policy deductible requires the general contractor to share the financial responsibility with the insurance company.

14. Answer: c) Provides protection against financial losses from subcontractor default

    Explanation: SDI provides protection for general contractors against financial losses in the event of subcontractor default.

15. Answer: d) Allocates certain risks to another party

    Explanation: Contractual indemnity allocates certain risks to another party, providing risk management benefits.

16. Answer: c) Identifies and evaluates potential risks

    Explanation: Risk assessment tools help identify and evaluate potential risks, allowing for proactive risk management.

17. Answer: d) Prevents the insurance company from suing subcontractors

    Explanation: A waiver of subrogation prevents the insurance company from suing subcontractors for damages covered by the policy.

18. Answer: c) Reduces the impact of unforeseen events

    Explanation: A crisis management plan helps reduce the impact of unforeseen events, contributing to effective risk management.

19. Answer: d) Requires the general contractor to comply with specified insurance requirements

    Explanation: The project owner may require the general contractor to comply with specific insurance requirements as part of risk transfer.

20. Answer: c) Defining requirements for builder's risk insurance

    Explanation: The Missouri Builders' Risk Insurance Act defines requirements related to builder's risk insurance in the state.

21. Answer: c) Provides a systematic approach to identify, assess, and manage risks

    Explanation: A risk register provides a systematic approach to identify, assess, and manage risks on a construction project.

22. Answer: b) Prevents recovery of economic losses through tort claims

    Explanation: The Economic Loss Doctrine may prevent the recovery of economic losses through tort claims, influencing risk management strategies.

23. Answer: c) Provides a structured approach to identify, assess, and respond to risks

    Explanation: A risk management plan provides a structured approach to identify, assess, and respond to risks on a construction project.

24. Answer: b) Certifies completion of the project

    Explanation: Performance bonds certify the general contractor's commitment to completing the project according to the terms of the contract.

25. Answer: c) Provides financial protection against unforeseen events

    Explanation: Insurance coverage provides financial protection against unforeseen events and is a key component of effective risk management for general contractors.

PART-NINE

Technology in Construction Answer

1. Answer: b) Provides a 3D representation of the construction project

   Explanation: BIM provides a 3D representation of the construction project, facilitating better visualization and coordination.

2. Answer: b) Aiding in site surveys, inspections, and monitoring

   Explanation: Drones can aid in site surveys, inspections, and monitoring, enhancing efficiency and safety.

3. Answer: b) Automates project management tasks

   Explanation: Construction management software automates various project management tasks, improving efficiency and organization.

4. Answer: c) Overlapping virtual information onto the physical construction site

   Explanation: AR overlays virtual information onto the physical construction site, aiding in design visualization and coordination.

5. Answer: c) Accelerates project schedules and reduces on-site work

   Explanation: Prefabrication and modular construction can accelerate project schedules and reduce on-site work through off-site fabrication.

6. Answer: b) Creating physical objects layer by layer from digital models

   Explanation: 3D printing creates physical objects layer by layer from digital models, allowing for innovative construction methods.

7. Answer: b) Enhances collaboration among project stakeholders

   Explanation: VR enhances collaboration by providing immersive experiences for project stakeholders, improving understanding and decision-making.

8. Answer: b) Aiding in accurate as-built documentation and site measurements

   Explanation: Laser scanning technology aids in accurate as-built documentation and site measurements, improving precision in construction.

9. Answer: b) Streamlines communication and access to project information

   Explanation: Mobile construction apps streamline communication and provide easy access to project information, improving efficiency.

10. Answer: b) Aiding in site selection and analysis

    Explanation: GIS technology can aid in site selection and analysis, providing valuable geographic information for construction projects.

11. Answer: b) Streamlining communication and collaboration among project team members

    Explanation: Real-time project collaboration platforms streamline communication and collaboration among project team members.

12. Answer: b) Automating repetitive and labor-intensive tasks

    Explanation: Construction Robotics automates repetitive and labor-intensive tasks, improving efficiency and safety.

13. Answer: b) Connecting and collecting data from construction equipment and devices

    Explanation: IoT technology connects and collects data from construction equipment and devices, improving data-driven decision-making.

14. Answer: b) Provides real-time health monitoring and safety alerts

    Explanation: Wearable technology provides real-time health monitoring and safety alerts for construction workers.

15. Answer: b) Streamlining project management tasks and processes

    Explanation: A Construction PMIS streamlines project management tasks and processes, improving overall project efficiency.

16. Answer: b) Analyzing data to predict project outcomes and optimize decision-making

    Explanation: Machine Learning and AI can analyze data to predict project outcomes and optimize decision-making in construction.

17. Answer: b) Tracking and managing construction materials and equipment

    Explanation: RFID technology tracks and manages construction materials and equipment, improving site management.

18. Answer: b) Providing a centralized platform for data storage and collaboration

    Explanation: Cloud computing provides a centralized platform for data storage and collaboration in construction projects.

19. Answer: b) Providing precise and detailed site measurements

    Explanation: Advanced surveying technologies provide precise and detailed site measurements, improving accuracy in construction.

20. Answer: b) Enhancing visualization of project plans and designs

    Explanation: Project Visualization Software enhances the visualization of project plans and designs, aiding in communication.

21. Answer: b) Increasing the speed and efficiency of construction tasks

    Explanation: Automated equipment and robotics can increase the speed and efficiency of various construction tasks.

22. Answer: b) Monitoring and managing environmental impacts

    Explanation: Environmental Monitoring Technology helps monitor and manage environmental impacts during construction projects.

23. Answer: b) Providing real-time data and diagnostics for construction equipment

    Explanation: Smart Construction Equipment provides real-time data and diagnostics, improving the efficiency of construction equipment.

24. Answer: b) Enhances collaboration among project stakeholders

    Explanation: Collaborative project delivery methods enhance collaboration among various project stakeholders.

25. Answer: b) Providing immersive training experiences for construction tasks

    Explanation: AR can provide immersive training experiences for construction workers, aiding in skill development and safety training.

PART-TEN

Emerging Trends and Innovations Answer

1. Answer: c) Accelerates project schedules and reduces on-site work

    Explanation: Prefabrication and modular construction can accelerate project schedules and reduce on-site work through off-site fabrication.

2. Answer: c) Enhances environmental responsibility and lowers operating costs

    Explanation: Sustainable building practices enhance environmental responsibility and can lower operating costs over the building's lifecycle.

3. Answer: a) Replacing traditional communication methods

    Explanation: 5G technology can replace traditional communication methods, providing faster and more reliable data transfer.

4. Answer: d) Offering visual overlays of project information on the physical site

    Explanation: AR offers visual overlays of project information on the physical construction site, aiding in design and coordination.

5. Answer: c) Enhances data-driven decision-making and project optimization

    Explanation: AI integration in construction management enhances data-driven decision-making and project optimization.

6. Answer: c) Aiding in site surveys, inspections, and monitoring

   Explanation: Drones can aid in site surveys, inspections, and monitoring, improving efficiency and safety.

7. Answer: c) Enhances transparency, security, and efficiency in project transactions

   Explanation: Blockchain technology enhances transparency, security, and efficiency in project transactions and documentation.

8. Answer: c) Enhances collaboration and coordination among project stakeholders

   Explanation: BIM enhances collaboration and coordination by providing a shared 3D model of the construction project.

9. Answer: c) Automating repetitive and labor-intensive tasks to improve efficiency

   Explanation: Robotics can automate repetitive and labor-intensive tasks, improving efficiency and safety on construction sites.

10. Answer: c) Connects and collects data from construction equipment and devices

    Explanation: IoT technology connects and collects data from construction equipment and devices, improving data-driven decision-making.

11. Answer: c) Allows for innovative and customized construction materials

    Explanation: 3D printing allows for the creation of innovative and customized construction materials.

12. Answer: c) Provides real-time data and diagnostics for construction equipment

    Explanation: Smart Construction Equipment provides real-time data and diagnostics, improving the efficiency of construction tasks.

13. Answer: b) Enhance collaboration among project stakeholders

    Explanation: Collaborative project delivery methods enhance collaboration among various project stakeholders.

14. Answer: c) Automates tasks such as excavation and material handling

    Explanation: Autonomous Construction Vehicles can automate tasks such as excavation and material handling, improving efficiency.

15. Answer: c) Improves project efficiency and reduces waste

    Explanation: Lean Construction principles aim to improve project efficiency and reduce waste in construction processes.

16. Answer: c) Analyzes data to predict project outcomes and optimize decision-making

    Explanation: Predictive Analytics analyzes data to predict project outcomes and optimize decision-making in construction.

17. Answer: c) Automates routine and repetitive administrative tasks

    Explanation: RPA can automate routine and repetitive administrative tasks, improving efficiency.

18. Answer: c) Monitors and manages environmental impacts, promoting sustainability

    Explanation: Environmental Monitoring Technology helps monitor and manage environmental impacts, promoting sustainability in construction.

19. Answer: c) Aims to minimize waste and promote the reuse of materials

    Explanation: The Circular Economy concept aims to minimize waste and promote the reuse of materials in construction practices.

20. Answer: c) Enhances real-time communication and collaboration among project team members

    Explanation: Real-time Project Collaboration Platforms enhance real-time communication and collaboration among project team members.

21. Answer: c) Enhances worker capabilities through technology

    Explanation: Human Augmentation Technology can enhance worker capabilities through the use of technology.

22. Answer: c) Provides precise and detailed site measurements, improving accuracy

    Explanation: Advanced surveying technologies provide precise and detailed site measurements, improving accuracy in construction.

23. Answer: c) Predicts when equipment maintenance is needed, minimizing downtime

    Explanation: Predictive Maintenance predicts when equipment maintenance is needed, minimizing downtime and improving efficiency.

24. Answer: c) Encourages sustainable and environmentally friendly construction practices

    Explanation: Green Building Certification encourages sustainable and environmentally friendly construction practices.

25. Answer: c) Creates a digital replica of the physical construction project for analysis and optimization

    Explanation: Digital Twins create a digital replica of the physical construction project for analysis and optimization, improving project management.

PART-ELEVEN

Common Challenges Faced by General Contractors Answer

1. Answer: b) Inaccurate cost estimation

   Explanation: Inaccurate cost estimation can lead to financial challenges for general contractors during the bidding process.

2. Answer: b) Causes delays and disruptions

   Explanation: Weather conditions can cause delays and disruptions, affecting the timeline of construction projects in Missouri.

3. Answer: c) Subcontractor default or non-performance

   Explanation: Subcontractor default or non-performance is a common risk that can affect general contractors in Missouri.

4. Answer: c) Increases the risk of legal issues

   Explanation: Changing regulatory requirements can increase the risk of legal issues and compliance challenges for general contractors.

5. Answer: b) Difficulty in securing adequate project financing

   Explanation: Difficulty in securing adequate project financing is a common issue faced by general contractors in Missouri.

6. Answer: c) Result in increased labor costs and project delays

   Explanation: Labor shortages can result in increased labor costs and project delays for general contractors.

7. Answer: c) Poses a learning curve and implementation challenges

   Explanation: The adoption of technology may pose a learning curve and implementation challenges for general contractors.

8. Answer: c) Leads to misunderstandings and project delays

   Explanation: The lack of effective communication can lead to misunderstandings and project delays for general contractors.

9. Answer: b) Inefficient use of resources

   Explanation: Inefficient use of resources is a common challenge in project scheduling for general contractors.

10. Answer: c) Result in uncertainty, affecting project demand and financing

    Explanation: Economic fluctuations can result in uncertainty, affecting project demand and financing for general contractors.

11. Answer: b) Increased risk of accidents and injuries

    Explanation: Safety compliance challenges may lead to an increased risk of accidents and injuries for general contractors.

12. Answer: c) Leads to subpar construction quality

    Explanation: The lack of skilled labor can lead to subpar construction quality for general contractors.

13. Answer: b) Insufficient record-keeping and documentation

    Explanation: Insufficient record-keeping and documentation can pose challenges for general contractors.

14. Answer: b) Increases the risk of legal disputes and associated costs

    Explanation: The risk of construction litigation can increase the likelihood of legal disputes and associated costs for general contractors.

15. Answer: b) Difficulty in managing and accommodating frequent scope changes

    Explanation: Managing and accommodating frequent scope changes can be a common challenge for general contractors.

16. Answer: c) Pose a risk of delays and quality issues

    Explanation: Subcontractor performance can pose a risk of delays and quality issues for general contractors.

17. Answer: b) Difficulty in sourcing quality materials and services

    Explanation: Difficulty in sourcing quality materials and services is a common challenge in project procurement for general contractors.

18. Answer: b) Increases the risk of unforeseen challenges and financial losses

    Explanation: The lack of effective risk management can increase the risk of unforeseen challenges and financial losses for general contractors.

19. Answer: c) Poses a risk of project delays and legal hurdles

    Explanation: Community opposition or public resistance can pose a risk of project delays and legal hurdles for general contractors.

20. Answer: c) Increases the risk of inefficiencies and errors

    Explanation: The lack of standardized processes can increase the risk of inefficiencies and errors for general contractors.

21. Answer: b) Difficulty in maintaining consistent quality standards

    Explanation: Difficulty in maintaining consistent quality standards can be a challenge for general contractors in project quality control.

22. Answer: c) Introduce uncertainties affecting material costs and project timelines

    Explanation: Geopolitical factors can introduce uncertainties affecting material costs and project timelines for general contractors.

23. Answer: b) Difficulty in managing multiple subcontractors and schedules

    Explanation: Coordinating multiple subcontractors and schedules can be a common challenge for general contractors.

24. Answer: c) Increases the risk of falling behind in competitiveness

    Explanation: The lack of innovative technologies can increase the risk of falling behind in competitiveness for general contractors.

25. Answer: b) Difficulty in resolving outstanding issues and obtaining project sign-off

    Explanation: Difficulty in resolving outstanding issues and obtaining project sign-off can be a challenge in project closeout for general contractors.

PART-TWELEVE

Case Studies Answer

1. Answer: a) Inefficient project management

   Explanation: Inefficient project management might contribute to delays in handling unexpected issues like severe weather conditions.

2. Answer: c) Changing project scope

   Explanation: Changes in project scope can lead to cost overruns if not adequately managed.

3. Answer: c) Insufficient contract documentation

   Explanation: Insufficient contract documentation can lead to legal disputes with subcontractors.

4. Answer: c) Lack of community engagement

   Explanation: Lack of community engagement can contribute to community opposition during construction projects.

5. Answer: b) Changing regulatory requirements

   Explanation: Changes in regulatory requirements can lead to delays in project approvals.

6. Answer: b) Lack of adherence to safety regulations

   Explanation: Non-compliance with safety regulations can lead to safety issues on construction sites.

7. Answer: c) Lack of due diligence in subcontractor evaluation

   Explanation: Insufficient evaluation of subcontractors can lead to performance challenges.

8. Answer: c) Unstable economic conditions

   Explanation: Unstable economic conditions can make it challenging to secure project financing.

9. Answer: d) Insufficient change order processes

   Explanation: Inadequate change order processes can lead to disputes related to project scope changes.

10. Answer: d) Lack of standardized processes

    Explanation: The absence of standardized processes can impact quality control in construction projects.

11. Answer: c) Lack of alignment with community needs

    Explanation: Lack of alignment with community needs can hinder community collaboration.

12. Answer: b) Unstable political situations

    Explanation: Unstable political situations can lead to delays due to geopolitical factors.

13. Answer: c) Lack of standardized processes

    Explanation: The absence of standardized processes can hinder subcontractor coordination.

14. Answer: c) Lack of awareness and resistance to change

    Explanation: Lack of awareness and resistance to change can hinder innovation adoption.

15. Answer: a) Efficient resolution of outstanding issues

    Explanation: Efficient resolution of outstanding issues is crucial for a smooth project closeout.

PART-FOURTEEN

Future Outlook of the Construction Industry Answer

1. Answer: b) Advancements in construction technology

   Explanation: Advancements in construction technology are a key driver shaping the future of the construction industry, improving efficiency and processes.

2. Answer: c) Enhances long-term viability and resilience

   Explanation: The adoption of sustainable practices enhances the long-term viability and resilience of the construction industry.

3. Answer: c) Fosters innovation and addresses labor shortages

   Explanation: Workforce diversity fosters innovation and helps address labor shortages in the construction industry.

4. Answer: c) Enhances project efficiency and coordination

   Explanation: BIM enhances project efficiency and coordination through the use of a shared 3D model.

5. Answer: c) Improves project efficiency and reduces on-site work

   Explanation: Off-site construction methods improve project efficiency and reduce on-site work, accelerating project schedules.

6. Answer: b) Enhances worker safety and efficiency

    Explanation: Robotics in construction enhances worker safety and efficiency, transforming the future workforce.

7. Answer: c) Promotes sustainable and energy-efficient construction

    Explanation: Renewable energy integration promotes sustainable and energy-efficient construction practices.

8. Answer: c) Enhances project design and visualization capabilities

    Explanation: AR enhances project design and visualization capabilities, aiding in communication and decision-making.

9. Answer: c) Enhances real-time communication and collaboration

    Explanation: 5G technology enhances real-time communication and collaboration among project stakeholders.

10. Answer: c) Enhances data-driven decision-making and project optimization

    Explanation: AI enhances data-driven decision-making and project optimization in construction management.

11. Answer: c) Accelerates project schedules and reduces on-site work

    Explanation: Prefabrication and modular construction accelerate project schedules and reduce on-site work.

12. Answer: c) Connects and collects data from construction equipment and devices

    Explanation: IoT connects and collects data from construction equipment and devices, improving data-driven decision-making.

13. Answer: c) Encourages sustainable and environmentally friendly construction practices

    Explanation: Sustainability certifications like LEED encourage sustainable and environmentally friendly construction practices.

14. Answer: c) Aids in site surveys, inspections, and monitoring

    Explanation: Drones can aid in site surveys, inspections, and monitoring, improving efficiency and safety.

15. Answer: c) Enhances transparency, security, and efficiency in project transactions

    Explanation: Blockchain technology enhances transparency, security, and efficiency in project transactions and documentation.

16. Answer: a) Reduces the need for on-site construction

    Explanation: 3D printing technology can reduce the need for traditional on-site construction methods.

17. Answer: c) Aims to minimize waste and promote the reuse of materials

    Explanation: The Circular Economy approach aims to minimize waste and promote the reuse of materials in construction.

18. Answer: b) Adoption of workforce development programs and training initiatives

    Explanation: The future of construction involves adopting workforce development programs to address skilled labor shortages.

19. Answer: c) Enhances project resilience to natural disasters and external shocks

    Explanation: Resilience planning enhances a project's ability to withstand natural disasters and external shocks.

20. Answer: c) Enhances efficiency through interconnected urban infrastructure

    Explanation: Smart cities concepts enhance efficiency through interconnected urban infrastructure.

21. Answer: b) Encourage sustainable and innovative construction practices

    Explanation: Government policies and incentives can encourage sustainable and innovative construction practices in the future.

22. Answer: c) Addresses evolving skill requirements and enhances workforce capabilities

    Explanation: Reskilling and upskilling initiatives address evolving skill requirements and enhance workforce capabilities.

23. Answer: c) Creates a digital replica of the physical construction project for analysis and optimization

    Explanation: Digital twins create a digital replica of the physical construction project for analysis and optimization, improving project management.

24. Answer: c) Streamlines processes and reduces waste

    Explanation: Lean construction principles aim to streamline processes and reduce waste in construction projects.

25. Answer: c) Introduces uncertainties and requires adaptability

    Explanation: Global trends and market dynamics introduce uncertainties, requiring adaptability for future competitiveness in the construction industry.

PART-FIFTEEN

General contractor Mathematics Calculations Answer

1. Answer: a) Volume = length × width × height

   Explanation: The formula for the volume of a rectangular prism is length multiplied by width multiplied by height.

2. Answer: a) 1,000 cubic feet

   Explanation: The total cubic footage is calculated as length × width × height, so 15 feet × 10 feet × 8 feet = 1,200 cubic feet.

3. Answer: c) 48 feet

   Explanation: The perimeter of a square is the sum of all four sides, which in this case is 4 × side length (4 × 12 = 48 feet).

4. Answer: c) $1,500

   Explanation: The area of the floor is 20 feet × 15 feet = 300 square feet. Multiplying the area by the cost per square foot gives $6 × 300 = $1,800.

5. Answer: b) 20%

   Explanation: The percentage decrease is calculated as [(Old Value - New Value) / Old Value] × 100, so [(80,000 - 64,000) / 80,000] × 100 = 20%.

6. Answer: c) 60%

   Explanation: The percentage completed is calculated as [(Weeks Completed / Total Weeks) × 100], so (10 / 15) × 100 = 60%.

7. Answer: b) 0.67

   Explanation: The slope (or pitch) is calculated as the rise divided by the run, so 6 feet / 9 feet = 0.67.

8. Answer: b) 4

   Explanation: The number of trucks needed is the total volume required divided by the volume each truck can carry, so 25 cubic yards / 5 cubic yards per truck = 4 trucks.

9. Answer: a) $1,500

   Explanation: The weekly earnings are calculated as the hourly rate multiplied by the number of hours worked, so $30 × 50 = $1,500.

10. Answer: c) 13

    Explanation: The square root of 169 is the number that, when multiplied by itself, equals 169. In this case, $\sqrt{169} = 13$.

11. Answer: b) $25,000

    Explanation: The total project cost is the sum of the cost of materials and labor, so $10,000 + $15,000 = $25,000.

12. Answer: c) 80%

    Explanation: The percentage of completion is calculated as (Hours Completed / Total Budgeted Hours) × 100, so (480 / 600) × 100 = 80%.

13. Answer: a) 45 square feet

    Explanation: The area of a triangle is calculated as (Base × Height) / 2, so (15 × 9) / 2 = 45 square feet.

14. Answer: b) 1 foot on the blueprint represents 75 feet in reality

    Explanation: The scale 1:75 means that every unit on the blueprint represents 75 of the same unit in reality.

15. Answer: a) 5

    Explanation: The number of trucks needed is the total volume required divided by the volume each truck can carry, so 30 cubic yards / 6 cubic yards per truck = 5 trucks.

16. Answer: b) 40 units

    Explanation: The perimeter of a triangle is the sum of its three sides, so 8 + 15 + 17 = 40 units.

17. Answer: b) 20%

    Explanation: The percentage increase is calculated as [(New Duration - Original Duration) / Original Duration] × 100, so [(15 - 12) / 12] × 100 = 25%.

18. Answer: a) Circumference = π × diameter

    Explanation: The formula for the circumference of a circle is π × diameter.

19. Answer: c) 5

    Explanation: The number of trucks needed is the total weight required divided by the weight each truck can carry, so 20 tons / 4 tons per truck = 5 trucks.

20. Answer: b) 2

    Explanation: The slope (m) of a line passing through two points (x_1, y_1) and (x_2, y_2) is calculated as $(y_2 - y_1) / (x_2 - x_1)$, so $(10 - 6) / (5 - 3) = 2$.

21. Answer: a) 16.67

    Explanation: The volume of concrete is calculated as (Length × Width × Depth) / 27 (to convert cubic feet to cubic yards), so (25 × 35 × 0.67) / 27 = 16.67 cubic yards.

22. Answer: c) Area = π × radius²

    Explanation: The formula for the area of a circle is π × radius squared.

23. Answer: c) 1,200

    Explanation: The total square footage covered is the quantity of paint multiplied by the coverage per gallon, so 8 gallons × 150 square feet per gallon = 1,200 square feet.

24. Answer: c) Determining the hypotenuse of a right-angled triangle

    Explanation: The Pythagorean Theorem is used to find the length of the hypotenuse in a right-angled triangle.

25. Answer: a) Missouri Department of Commerce and Insurance

    Explanation: The Missouri Department of Commerce and Insurance is responsible for licensing general contractors in the state.

26. Explanation: The formula for calculating the load-bearing capacity of a beam is Load ÷ Area.**

27. Explanation: The formula for calculating the area of a rectangular room is Length × Width.

28. Explanation: The formula for calculating the volume of a rectangular prism is Length × Width × Height.

29. Explanation: The constant used for the mathematical formula to calculate the area of a circle is π (pi).

30. Explanation: The Pythagorean Theorem is used for determining angles in right-angled triangles.

31. Explanation: The slope of a roof is expressed mathematically as Rise/Run.

32. Explanation: The "cut and fill" calculation is used for determining the volume of soil to be removed or added during site grading.

33. Explanation: The trapezoidal rule for calculating the area of an irregular shape is (Base1 + Base2) × Height ÷ 2.

34. Explanation: The formula for calculating the volume of a cylinder is $\pi r^2 h$, where r is the radius and h is the height.

35. Explanation: Unit rate in construction cost estimation refers to the cost per unit of measurement, such as cost per square foot or cost per linear foot.

36. Explanation: The formula for calculating the perimeter of a rectangle is 2 × (Length + Width).

37. Explanation: The formula for calculating concrete volume for a circular column is $\pi r^2 h$, where r is the radius and h is the height.

38. Explanation: The "net present value" (NPV) is used in financial analysis to evaluate the profitability of construction projects over time.

39. Explanation: The surface area of a cylinder is calculated as $2\pi r^2 + 2\pi rh$, where r is the radius and h is the height.

40. Explanation: The critical path in construction project scheduling represents the longest path to completion, determining the project's overall duration.

41. Explanation: Percent slope represents the angle of inclination in construction calculations.

42. Explanation: The formula for calculating the area of a triangle is (Base × Height) ÷ 2.

43. Explanation: The "moment of inertia" calculation in structural engineering is used for evaluating a structure's resistance to bending.

44. Explanation: The cost of concrete is calculated as Volume × Unit Price.

45. Explanation: The formula for calculating the total cost of labor is Hours × Rate.

46. Explanation: The aspect ratio of a rectangular shape is calculated as Length ÷ Width.

47. Explanation: The "pitch" calculation for a roof is used for determining roof slope.

48. Explanation: The formula for calculating the area of a trapezoid is (Base1 + Base2) ÷ 2 × Height.

49. Explanation: The cost of materials is calculated as Quantity × Unit Price.

50. Explanation: Linear feet refers to the measurement of length, often used for things like baseboards, trim, or fencing.

Made in the USA
Columbia, SC
13 March 2025